Bring Forth Your
LIGHT

Bring Forth Your
LIGHT

All Things Are
POSSIBLE

Frederick & June Babbel

ISBN: 1-55517-355-1

10 9 8 7 6 5 4 3 2 1

Published and Distributed by:

925 North Main, Springville, UT 84663 • 801/489-4084

CFI
Publishing and
Distribution Since 1986

Cedar Fort, Incorporated

CFI Distribution • CFI Books • Inside Cougar Report

Cover design and page layout by Corinne A. Bischoff
Printed in the United States of America

Contents

Acknowledgments

Sincere gratitude and appreciation are due many people who offered meaningful suggestions and continued encouragement in the writing of this book. Choice friends and associates have painstakingly read and reviewed this manuscript. Special thanks are due to my devoted wife, June, whose constant assistance and valued partnership have contributed much.

Patience has been a special virtue in the complete support, encouragement, and assistance of the staff at CFI.

Introduction

Due to the enthusiastic response of readers to my earlier books, *On Wings of Faith* and *To Him That Believeth*, I have been encouraged to write another inspirational book, one which focuses upon vital matters that confront us daily.

For years many of those who have heard me speak have urged me to write forthrightly about divine commandments and principles that have been given to fortify us in establishing and pursuing a life in accordance with God's plan for our joy and eternal welfare. With this book I am responding to that challenge.

One evening during the Christmas holidays I had been seriously considering the subject and title of such a book. In the dreams or visions of the night I heard the beautiful strains of an angelic chours of little children singing two familiar songs with such earnestness and feeling that I found myself shedding tears of gratitude and joy. For the first time in my life the poignant messages of these songs burst upon me. They emphasize the need for developing our own personal divine light, and expanding it by caring enough to share it with others.

This same vision and heavenly singing was repeated again just four days after the New Year. This time these songs made an even greater impact. Why should this divine recital have been repeated?

As I was pondering this event, I heard a most pleasing voice saying, "The title of the book you have been invited to write should be *Bring Forth Your Light!*

Two Primary songs beautifully express our need to be "the light of the world" and to serve others. May I share the words of these songs with you? I remember singing them joyfully when I was a little child in Primary.

Shine On

My light is but a little one,
My light of faith and prayer;
But lo! it glows like God's great sun,
For it was lighted there.
I may not hide my little light;
The Lord has told me so.
'Tis given me to keep in sight,
That all may see it glow.

Shine on, shine on, shine on bright and clear;
Shine on, shine on now the day is here.

The second memorable song is an appeal for caring and sharing —the essence of divine love:

"Give," Said the Little Stream

"Give," said the little stream,
"Give, oh! give, give, oh! give."
"Give," said the little stream,
As it hurried down the hill;
"I'm small, I know, but wherever I go
The fields grow greener still."

"Give," said the little rain,
"Give, oh! give, give, oh! give."
"Give," said the little rain,
As it fell upon the flow'rs;
"I'll raise their drooping heads again,"
As it fell upon the flow'rs.

Give, then, as Jesus gives,
Give, oh! give, give, oh! give.
Give, then, as Jesus gives;
There is something all can give.
Do as the streams and blossoms do:

For God and others live.

Singing, singing all the day,
"Give away, oh! give away."
Singing, singing all the day,
"Give, oh! give away."

(*Children's Songbook* [Salt Lake City: The Church of Jesus Christ of Latter-day Saints, 1989], pp. 144, 236.)

The messages of these two simple but impressive songs illustrate vividly the principles that the Lord would have us manifest in our daily living.

These principles form the basis of this book. We need to bring forth our own light and share it lovingly and abundantly with those who are "hungering and thirsting after righteousness."

chapter one

Where there is no vision, the people perish.
— Proverbs 29:18

Bring Forth Your Light

The present state of our world is like no other in the history of mankind.* The need for Latter-day Saints to be faithful and prepared is abundantly clear.

Elder Vaughn J. Featherstone of the First Quorum of Seventy plainly warned: "Satan has unleashed every evil, every scheme, every blatant and vile perversion ever known to man in any generation. Just as this is the dispensation of the fulness of times, it is also the dispensation of the fulness of evil. We and our wives and husbands, our children, and our members must find safety. There is no safety in the world; wealth cannot provide it, enforcement agencies cannot assure it, membership in this Church alone cannot bring it...Let us prepare then [ourselves and our children] with the faith to surmount every trial and every condition." (From an address delivered 1 June 1987, Seattle, Washington.)

Our daily newspapers and our magazines confirm this voice of warning. Shameful and unspeakable corruption

---

* Note: *the first sentence of Vaughn J. Featherstone's quote is: "The season of the world before us will be like no other in the history of mankind.*

and violence are manifest in nearly all parts of our world. Prophecies and warnings from all ages are being fulfilled before our very eyes.

What is our hope? What course must we pursue to avoid or prevent these perversions, calamities, scourges, and plagues?

Our Eternal Father has always been vitally concerned for his children. In Old Testament times he admonished his people: "Train up a child in the way he should go: and when he is old, he will not depart from it" (Proverbs 22:6).

In 1833 the Lord gave similar counsel for our day:

> Light and truth forsake that evil one....
>
> I have commanded you to bring up your children in light and truth....
>
> You have not taught your children light and truth, according to the commandments; and that wicked one hath power, as yet, over you, and this is the cause of your affliction.
>
> And now a commandment I give unto you—if you will be delivered you shall set in order your own house, for there are many things that are not right in your house....
>
> What I say unto one I say unto all; pray always lest that wicked one have power in you (D&C 93:37-49).

The questions may arise, "How is it possible for us to fulfill these commandments if we don't even know what light and truth mean or how to obtain them? How can we teach something we do not understand?" It is the purpose of this book to help answer such questions.

We should first understand that light and darkness cannot exist in the same place at the same time. This is easily demonstrated by going into a dark room and then turning on the light. The darkness disappears. Where did it go? It has been replaced by the light. Where there is light, there is no darkness.

We do not have malicious intentions when we leave our children in darkness at night. If they are afraid of the dark, we might turn on a light and explain to them why they have no need to fear. We should also have a keen awareness that our children need not remain in spiritual darkness. When they come to us in fear or trouble, we should realize that the counsel we give them may have eternal consequences in their lives.

These observations represent our general understanding of light and truth. But what do these terms mean specifically in a scriptural context? Are light and truth things we can acquire? If so, how may we receive and internalize them?

What Is Light?

The word *light* has varied meanings in the scriptures. However, a common thread runs throughout the scriptures regarding the divine source of that light. The Psalmist wrote: "The Lord is my light and my salvation" (Psalm 27:1). Jesus declared: "I am the true light that lighteth every man that cometh into the world" (D&C 93:2). Having confounded the scribes and Pharisees who sought to stone the woman taken in adultery, Jesus declared: "I am the light of the world: he that followeth me shall not walk in darkness, but shall have the light of life" (John 8:12).

These and many other scriptures suggest, then, that all light must have a source of power. In this context *light* means literally the power of God. It is the perfecting power of God, the power necessary to shape our lives—our thoughts, our feelings, and our actions—in the divine pattern that Jesus so gloriously exemplified.

Section 88 of the Doctrine and Covenants provides added insight regarding this concept: "Which light proceedeth forth from the presence of God to fill the immensity of space—the light which is in all things, which giveth life to all things, which is the law by which all things are governed, even the power of God who sitteth upon his throne, who is in the bosom of eternity, who is in the midst of all things" (D&C 88:12-13).

Our Savior's invitation to us is that we accept the power (light) which is his and which he is eager to share with us (see D&C 93:20). When we realize that the light he offers us is the same divine power by which all things were created, how can we possibly reject his invitation?

What Is Truth?

That we might better understand what *truth* is, Jesus clarified its basic meaning: "Truth is knowledge of things as they are, and as they were, and as they are to come" (D&C 93:24).

This statement signifies that truth is knowledge of things as they *really* are, were, or will be, not as people may say or believe they are. There is a marked difference. In the very next verse of this same section the Lord gives us a divine guideline to recognize this difference: "And whatsoever is more or less than this is the spirit of that wicked one who was a liar from the beginning" (D&C 93:25).

By this standard only divine or divinely inspired knowledge and insight constitute *genuine* truth. Christ's mission and purpose from the very beginning—even before the foundation of this world was laid—were to exemplify and share such truth (divine knowledge) and light (power) as he received them from our Heavenly Father.

In summary, then, we may define these two terms as follows: *Light* is the power of God, and *truth* is the knowledge from God.

How May We Obtain Truth?

For us the resurrected Christ is our primary source of light, without which we are incapable of comprehending and applying successfully those principles of truth necessary for our salvation and eternal life.

He invites us to accept his teachings, which represent divine truth. In shaping our lives we should follow his guileless example as the embodiment of those truths. By so doing we are prepared to bring forth our own God-designed potential.

As we perceive, understand, and apply his truth, and as we are empowered to do so through his light, we gain experience and become increasingly capable of sharing this same light and truth with others. In such sharing we can actually benefit ourselves, receiving greater light and truth until we may encompass a fulness, as Christ does and all those will who truly accept and follow him.

The Prophet Joseph Smith counseled, "The best way to obtain truth and wisdom is not to ask it from books, but to go to God in prayer, and obtain divine teaching…. There is never a time when the spirit is too old to approach God." (*Teachings of the Prophet Joseph Smith,* comp. Joseph Fielding Smith [Salt Lake City: Deseret Book Co., 1976], p. 191.)

In addition he gave us insight concerning the use of the scriptures and modern revelation in our quest for obtaining truth:

> Search the scriptures—search the revelations which we publish, and ask your Heavenly Father, in the name of His Son Jesus Christ, to manifest the truth unto you, and if you do it with an eye single to His glory nothing doubting, He will answer you by the power of His Holy Spirit. You will then know for yourselves and not for another. You will not then be dependent on man for the knowledge of God; nor will there be any room for speculation. No; for when men receive their

5

instruction from Him that made them, they know how He will
save them (*Teachings of the Prophet Joseph Smith*, pp. 11-12).

In a related vein, President Brigham Young gave special instructions on how the holders of the priesthood may
know God's mind continually:

> An individual who holds a share in the Priesthood, and contin-
> ues faithful to his calling, who delights himself continually in
> doing the things God requires at his hands, and continues
> through life in the performance of every duty, will secure to
> himself not only the privilege of receiving, but the knowledge
> how to receive the things of God, that he may know the mind
> of God continually; and he will be enabled to discern between
> right and wrong, between the things of God and the things that
> are not of God. And the Priesthood—the Spirit that is within
> him, will continue to increase until it becomes like a fountain of
> living water; until it is like the tree of life; until it is one contin-
> ued source of intelligence and instruction to that individual
> (*Journal of Discourses* 3:192).

Since the Lord has commanded us to bring up our children in light and truth, it is interesting to note the Lord's use
of these terms in another scripture that we will now discuss.

The Glory of God

Many of us through the years have become acquainted
with the scriptural pronouncement which has been printed
on numerous pamphlets and has become a symbol at some
of our universities. You have seen and heard it many times:
"The glory of God is intelligence."

However, we sometimes fail to read this scripture
through to its conclusion. Unless we do so, we may not
understand just what the Lord means by "intelligence."
Here is his definition and the conclusion of the scripture:
...or, in other words, light and truth" (D&C 93:36).

What is he communicating to us? *Intelligence* and *light*

and *truth* are synonyms for *the glory of God.*

When we are commanded to bring up our children in light and truth, then, we are commanded to bring them up to partake of the glory of God. In other words, we are commanded to bring up our children in a home where the power of God is manifest and the knowledge from God is a reality, exemplified and taught by parents who are applying these principles in their own lives.

This is light and truth—or glory—in action.

In a home where such glory is present, love and power and joy abound. In such a home, family members face and overcome problems through faith and prayer and trust in the Lord. It is not the quality of our possessions or even the neatness of our homes that will determine our children's capacity to partake of such glory. What a wonderful challenge and responsibility is thus entrusted to parents!

All of us should never underestimate the power of a good example—an inspiring role model. Those who are brought up in light and truth and are partakers of such glory manifest dynamic qualities that become an inspiration and challenge for others to equal. Well has the Psalmist declared, "For with thee is the fountain of life: in thy light shall we see light" (Psalm 36:9).

A noteworthy example of a servant of the Lord manifesting such light came to my attention in a rather unusual manner.

What Shall the Harvest Be?

After visiting with us in Salt Lake City, my parents left for their home in Twin Falls, Idaho. The snow was falling very heavily, and as they reached the Rattlesnake Pass between Tremonton and Snowville, Utah, they stopped to tighten their left rear tire chain. While my father was doing this, a drunk driver, coming down the hill from the opposite direction, struck and killed him.

After returning from the funeral, I was in the Lion House when a young man approached me and asked if I was the son of Frederick Babbel, about whom he had read in the newspaper. He invited me to join him, his father, and his brothers at their table.

The father related a thrilling bit of information about my father's priceless influence in their lives and the lives of many others.

After accepting the restored gospel, my father had emigrated in 1909 from East Prussia to the United States. He met my mother two years later, and they were married in the Salt Lake Temple. My mother was expecting her first child when he was called to serve as a missionary in Switzerland.

One of his first assignments was to labor in the Catholic canton of St. Gallen, Switzerland. With diligent effort he interested about thirty families in his message. However, they did not wish to make a commitment until they could arrange for him to meet with their priest in their presence, so they might determine for themselves whether or not the gospel message was true.

A suitable, large room was located for this purpose. When their priest arrived and was introduced to my father, the priest remarked, "This man is nothing but a tailor. He's not a priest at all!" He was assured that my father was a priest in his own church.

As they prepared for their discussion, my father suggested that they agree at the outset that the Spirit of Christ is the spirit of truth and that contention is of the devil. If they could conduct their discussion on this basis, he would be pleased to begin at once.

The priest was apparently taken off guard and hesitated for a moment. Then without a word he picked up his hat and left the room. The brother who was relating this event then told me, "I was one of those present. The next week your father baptized all of us. Before he left for another assignment, he was the director of a choir with nearly seventy-five members."

He also informed me that he and his sons had all been on missions. Their combined efforts had brought a substantial number of people into the Church. Many of these converts, in turn, had also been responsible for similar activities and success. He estimated that many hundreds of people had accepted the gospel message because of that early beginning, due to my father's willingness to share light and truth.

As we prepared to go our separate ways, this brother said, "Now that your father has been called home to his reward, he will be rejoicing to be greeted by many, many people who will thank him for having been the means of their receiving the restored gospel message."

These words penetrated my heart. I recalled my father's words the last evening he spent in our home. He said, in effect, "Every blessing I was promised in my patriarchal blessing has been literally fulfilled to the letter. If I could have one more wish, it would be to be called on another mission." I believe that the Lord granted him this wish.

How thankful I was to hear of my father's diligence in bringing forth the light! What a choice witness this was to me of the joy and success that attend those who seek to abide in light and truth—the glory of God! Never let it be said that one man abiding in God cannot make much difference.

God's Work and His Glory—Man

God is in the business of helping man help himself. He has already learned the lessons that we must learn for achieving perfection. His desire for us is reflected in the message that the Lord gave to Moses when this ancient prophet was "caught up into an exceedingly high mountain": "Behold, this is my work and my glory—to bring to pass the immortality and eternal life of man" (Moses 1:39).

His *work*—"to bring to pass the immortality...of man"—has been achieved and assured through the infinite atonement and resurrection wrought by Jesus, our Lord, our Savior, our Messiah. It is he to whom "every knee shall bow, and every tongue confess...that he is God" (Mosiah 27:31; see also Philippians 2:11 and Isaiah 45:23).

However, his glory in creation consists primarily in bringing to pass the "eternal life of man." He cannot do this without our cooperation. Eternal life is dependent upon our receiving and applying light and truth as he has commanded us to do, not only for our children's benefit but also for ourselves. If we fail to share in his glory we will not be able to realize his great desire for us, even eternal life, "which gift is the greatest of all the gifts of God" (D&C 14:7).

The testimony of John the Baptist describes how the Savior received a fulness of the Father's glory: "And I, John, bear record that I beheld his glory, as the glory of the Only Begotten of the Father.... And I, John, bear record that he received a fulness of the glory of the Father; and he received all power, both in heaven and on earth, and the glory of the Father was with him" (D&C 93:11, 16-17).

Even as our Heavenly Father has bestowed upon Jesus the fulness of his glory, so Jesus is also willing to share with us that light and truth until we may likewise receive a fulness of the glory of God.

Did not our Lord and Savior give us this divine promise? "For if you keep my commandments you shall receive of his fulness, and be glorified in me as I am in the Father" (D&C 93:20).

Similarly, John the Apostle gave us this great assurance: "Beloved, now are we the sons of God, and it doth not yet appear what we shall be: but we know that, when he shall appear, we shall be like him; for we shall see him as he is. And every man that hath this hope in him purifieth himself, even as he is pure" (1 John 3:2-3).

Those who gain eternal life through following the precepts and example of Jesus Christ will be enhancing the Savior's glory. "This is...my glory," he said, "to bring to pass the...eternal life of man" (Moses 1:39).

Then one day our Savior will be able to say to the Father not, "Here I am," but, "Here we are!" Oh, what joy will be ours that day, to realize that "we shall be like him"!

chapter two

Ye shall know them by their fruits
— Matthew 7:16

Developing the Light Within

There is great urgency today that each of us take an inventory of his spiritual condition. We have been fore-warned that we cannot live ultimately on borrowed light any more than could the five foolish virgins of Jesus' para-ble. Just as these five could not borrow oil from the five wise virgins in order to light their lamps, so we cannot borrow the personal spirituality required to gain an eternal reward.

If we could look at a meter—something that worked like a barometer—that would reflect the status of our divine light, where would we stand according to that meter today? Is our spirituality rising, or falling, or holding steady?

Sometimes we become so preoccupied with our work, our families, and our Church responsibilities that we rarely pause to reflect on our spiritual condition. If we did, we might ask some questions in the private recesses of our souls: Where am I now? How do I stand in relation to my divine potential as a child of God blessed with the restored gospel? Are my faith and testimony developing as they should?

The Light Within

In 1867 President Heber C. Kimball delivered a discourse

in which he made the following prophecy and admonition: "The time will come when no man nor woman will be able to endure on borrowed light. Each will have to be guided by the light within himself. If you do not have it, how can you stand?...You will be left to the light within yourselves. If you don't have it you will not stand; therefore seek for the testimony of Jesus and cleave to it, that when the trying time comes you may not stumble and fall" (As cited in Orson F. Whitney, *Life of Heber C. Kimball* [Salt Lake City: Bookcraft, 1967], p. 450).

Before Elder Harold B. Lee became President of the Church, he would sometimes go into the mission field and talk with the missionaries. To those who said they felt that they did not have powerful faith or a sure testimony, he would often say, "Let me bear you my testimony, and for the time being suppose you cling to my testimony until you develop one for yourself." Though Elder Lee offered to lend his light, as it were, for a time to these missionaries, he still emphasized their responsibility to gain their own portion of light.

In his book *Decisions for Successful Living* President Lee echoed Heber C. Kimball's words above and again stressed the need for members to gain personal testimonies: "I would fervently pray that you could feel the love flowing from my soul to yours, and know of my deep compassion toward each of you as you face your problems of the day. The time is here when every one of you must stand on your own feet. The time is here when no man and woman will endure on borrowed light. Each will have to be guided by the light within himself. If you do not have it, you will not stand" ([Salt Lake City: Deseret Book, 1973], p. 234).

In view of President Heber C. Kimball's prophecy and President Lee's declaration, we should actively pursue the quest for light and truth until we, too, have brought forth that "light within."

Guidelines for Bringing Forth the Light Within

In order for us to develop and bring forth the "light within" we would do well to consider the following guidelines:

1. *Hunger and thirst after righteousness.* "Blessed are all they who do hunger and thirst after righteousness, for they shall be filled with the Holy Ghost" (3 Nephi 12:6).

   The Prophet Joseph Smith invited us to perceive an even greater challenge and promise in connection with this principle: "Let [a person] continue to humble himself before God, hungering and thirsting after righteousness, and living by every word of God, and the Lord will soon say unto him, Son, thou shalt be exalted. When the Lord has thoroughly proved him, and finds that the man is determined to serve Him at all hazards, then the man will find his calling and his election made sure, then it will be his privilege to receive the other Comforter.... When any man obtains this last Comforter, he will have the personage of Jesus Christ to attend him" (*Teachings of the Prophet Joseph Smith*, pp. 150-51).

   The counsel of James can help us in our striving for righteousness: "Resist the devil, and he will flee from you. Draw nigh to God, and he will draw nigh to you" (James 4:7-8).

   In our day the Lord has emphasized the need for us to sincerely ask for spiritual guidance as we "hunger and thirst after righteousness": "If thou shalt ask, thou shalt receive revelation upon revelation, knowledge upon knowledge, that thou mayest know the mysteries and peaceable things—that which bringeth joy, that which bringeth life eternal" (D&C 42:61). The Lord has rich blessings in store for those who are truly seeking to bring forth their light.

2. *Seek the Spirit of the Lord.* If we are to bring forth our light, we will need the influence and guidance of the Spirit in our lives.

My wife, June, recalls her search for the Spirit of the Lord at a time when she was becoming so busy with her family and her other obligations that she felt she was starving spiritually much of the time. Here is her own account of that experience:

"I decided that having the Spirit of the Lord should at least make me happy. Peace of mind and gratitude and love should be further up the scale. On this basis I decided to find out how often I was 'in tune.' Whenever I thought about it, I would look at my watch and check my feelings. I would think, 'Ten thirty— no, not particularly happy,' or, 'Quarter past seven—yes, I am happy right now.'

"I was horrified to realize that, although I was doing everything I should as far as I knew, there were large gaps of time when I did not particularly feel the Spirit, when I was not really happy.

"I found myself waking during the night, my brain going over and over the problems of the coming day. I was able to block such thoughts out by repeating over and over in my mind, 'Father, let there be light within me! Fill me with the "pure love of Christ" ' (see Moroni 7:47-40).

"One Sunday morning during the sacrament I tried making the prayer more personal—to 'liken it unto myself' as Nephi suggested (see 1 Nephi 19:23). During the prayer, I repeated in my mind, 'I will always remember him! I will! I will! I *will* have his Spirit with me during the coming week!' There I sat on the front row of the chapel, tears running down my cheeks. I soon noticed a wonderful warm feeling, slowly moving from my feet to the top of my head. Slowly it receded, then came again. And again. Three times it felt as if I were being bathed in the Spirit of the Lord. It was a glorious feeling. I realized that I was being taught, in a way I would always remember, how the Spirit feels.

"Then came the day that was to change my life. I realized I had not felt the Spirit of the Lord for five days, and wondered what I could do about it. The Relief Society cultural refinement lesson had been interesting, but had not helped me in my quest. Afterwards I had to drive the car to go pick up my husband, who was at a location about fifteen minutes away. As I started the car, I automatically reached for the radio, as I had always done while driving. 'No, that won't help me,' I thought, and I turned it off. 'What can I do?' I prayed.

"I tried scriptures. I tried poetry. I tried hymns. 'If the way be full of trial, weary not' became a dirge rather than an encouragement. I tried 'Rest, rest for the weary' and 'peace, peace to the soul,' but that just made me tired. Then I remembered fragments of 'If With All Your Heart' and 'O, Divine Redeemer,' and that did it! I began singing bits and pieces out loud as I was driving, modifying the words to fit my needs:

Oh, that I knew...where I might find thee,
    That I might even come before Thy Presence!
Oh, that I knew...where I might find thee!

'If with all your heart ye truly seek me,
    Ye shall ever surely find me,'
Thus saith our God!

O, divine Redeemer! O, divine Redeemer!...
    I pray thee, grant me pardon, and remember not,
Remember not, O Lord, my sins!

"Suddenly I realized that I did not have to be perfect before the Lord could love me. He loves *me*. When I sensed the depth of his love for me, I was filled with love and gratitude for him.

"It was an incredible experience. I could hardly see the road for the tears. But that day I learned one of the most important lessons of my life. I learned that I could change my spirituality from 0 to 100 percent in ten minutes through something I could do myself. Prior to that time, I was keeping track and thinking, 'Tomorrow will be a better day.' But now I knew that there was something I could do about it, and I could change my feelings."

Note the path she took in order to have the Spirit with her: (a) There was a great desire in her heart to have the Spirit; (b) she prayed constantly for inspiration to know what she could do to receive the Spirit and for light to be able to block out negative thoughts; (c) she tried different actions that came to her mind; and (d) she did not stop trying until finally the blessing came. Thus it is that, if we are willing to take the necessary steps to have the Spirit and are persistent in taking those steps, inevitably our diligence will be rewarded with blessings of light and comfort from the Spirit of the Lord.

3. *Take one step at a time.* Although it is possible for a child in school to skip a grade if his intelligence and skills warrant it, it is not possible for us to skip any stage in our spiritual growth. Each step is necessary as a preparation for succeeding challenges. There are no short cuts in spiritual development. Each of us has to begin from where he is and then progress one step at a time. However, we can accelerate the process by genuinely desiring to progress and diligently applying truth as our understanding of it increases.

If the Lord is willing to share his glory with us, then, how do we receive that glory? The same way Jesus did—a bit at a time.

"And I, John, saw that he received not of the fulness at the first, but...*continued from grace to grace,* until he received a fulness" (D&C 93:12-13; italics added).

Jesus has repeatedly invited us, "Come, follow me." Obviously, if he received not a fulness at first, but "continued from grace to grace, until he received a fulness," we should realize that this is also the pathway we are to follow if we are to acquire a fulness even as he did.

Taking one step at a time is a key to help us progress in our efforts to bring forth our light. "That which is of God is lightCastles; and he that receiveth light, and continueth in God, receiveth more light; and that light groweth brighter and brighter until the perfect day" (D&C 50:24).

This gradual increase of light in a person's life can help expand his perspective. This principle was beautifully illustrated to me while I was serving as a missionary in the German-Austrian mission before World War II.

During a visit to Potsdam, near Berlin, my companion and I joined a group to take a tour of two majestic castles once owned by Frederick the Great. As tourists we were required to cover our shoes with special soft mittens so that we would not mar the highly polished floors of the main royal castle. Our guide escorted us from room to room and explained the purposes of each one as well as of the various artifacts.

Finally he led us toward the grand ballroom, where lavish receptions had been featured. As we followed him down the hallway, he lit a candle and extinguished all of the electric lights. Since this was Nazi Germany, a feeling of foreboding came over some of those in the group. They did not know why we were being left in almost total darkness, nor did they know what to expect.

We soon learned what the guide was up to. As we reached the ballroom, the massive doors were opened. An eerie feeling came over us as the flickering flame of the candle revealed shadowy figures that seemed to be moving. Our eyes became accustomed to the dim light, and our first impression was one of ornate spaciousness. We were able to identify marble statues and standing coats of armor holding various weapons of that period. We became aware that there were many priceless paintings and costly treasures in the room, which we hoped to examine more closely.

Small crystal border lights were then turned on. We gasped in amazement as the beauty and splendor of this room became more clearly visible. The addition of these lights resulted in a profusion of scintillating colors of brilliant hues dancing from the massive pillars supporting the roof. These pillars were studded with all manner of precious gemstones in a dazzling variety of tints and colors. I had never before seen anything so breathtaking!

Next our guide pressed a button, and suddenly the resplendent crystal chandeliers overhead shone forth with brilliance and beauty. Now the room looked almost like an aurora borealis, so startling were the darting shafts of colored light reflected from the many-faceted gemstones and the huge mirrors.

The guide pressed a final button, and then all of the elegant drapes were withdrawn to uncover the window walls on both sides and on the end of the room. Now added to all of this indoor beauty was the brilliance of the sunshine, and through the windows we could see the fleecy clouds, the exquisite floral gardens surrounding a picturesque lake. Behind this lake stretched the magnificent Sans Souci castle with its historic old windmill and its graceful trees.

The impact of this experience—witnessing how gradual increases of light can change the look and feeling of a scene from that of anxiety to increasing levels of interest, delight, and awesome splendor—changed my life and outlook. Since that day my search for light and truth has continued to grow. The memory of that overwhelming sight, which the withdrawing of the drapes presented to us that day, reminds me of this profound promise from Brigham Young: "When you shall have faith to rend that vail which is over your minds, you will find that the heavens are ready and waiting to bestow the blessings promised, just as soon as you are prepared to receive them" (*Journal of Discourses* 3:351).

Some among us seem to be content with a small candle. Others seem to be content with a ten-watt light bulb and rejoice that they can discern to some extent the plan of God. Those with increasingly brighter lights may be content with what they understand. Many fail to realize, however, that there is unlimited light available to those who are prepared to receive it.

4. *Keep moving toward your goal.* Be persistent.

Have you ever seen a battery-powered toy car try to make its way around a room? It goes forward as far as it can; when it meets an obstacle, it doesn't beat against it but tries to get around it. It backs up, adjusts its direction, and tries to move forward again. Over and over it stops when its way is blocked, backs up, and tries again until it finds a clear space where it can make progress.

Similarly we should be persistent in exercising our faith to overcome or "get around" our obstacles. We should never stop trying until we reach our goals.

The Lord has reminded us often that "he only is saved who endureth unto the end" (D&C 53:7). This involves persistence. Failing to thus endure, we may not only jeopardize our own salvation but also adversely affect our children's eternal welfare.

While we should persist in trying to gain our righteous goals, we also need to be patient with ourselves and our progress or we may become discouraged. We all need to learn different kinds of lessons, and sometimes it is as important to learn what does not work as to discover what does. By this we gain experience.

One young missionary who had a great desire to become perfect didn't understand the need for patience. He fasted and prayed occasionally and tried hard to be perfect. After three weeks trial, when he realized that he had not yet achieved perfection, he became discouraged and decided it was impossible. He stopped trying. His so-called "burning desire" needed more fuel. Perhaps he had never read the counsel of James: "The trying of your faith worketh patience. But let patience have her perfect work, that ye may be perfect and entire, wanting nothing" (James 1:3-4).

This missionary was on the right road and was headed in the right direction, but he stopped his efforts to reach his goal. To reach any goal requires persistence until you reach it. You never fail until you stop trying!

The prophet Nephi informed us of what we must do to inherit eternal life: "Wherefore, ye must *press forward* with a steadfastness in Christ, having a perfect brightness of hope, and a love of God and of all men. Wherefore, if ye shall press forward, feasting upon the word of Christ, and endure to the end, behold, thus saith the Father: ye shall have eternal life" (2 Nephi 31:20; italics added). Nephi's message is that we need to keep trying, keep hoping, keep loving, keep applying ourselves—and never give up. These are essential principles for us to follow in bringing forth our light.

5. *Keep the commandments.* The Lord has told us how we may receive light and truth: "He that keepeth his commandments receiveth truth and light, until he is glorified in truth and knoweth all things" (D&C 93:28). The Lord also has given us a warning: "If you keep not my commandments, the love of the Father shall not continue with you, therefore you shall walk in darkness" (D&C 95:12).

We all will be held accountable for our obedience or dis-obedience in relation to the commandments of God. We will also be held accountable for teaching or failing to teach our children to obey God's commandments. We would do well to ponder the Lord's words to Frederick G. Williams: "You have not taught your children light and truth, according to the commandments; and that wicked one hath power, as yet, over you, and this is the cause of your affliction. And now a commandment I give unto you—if you will be delivered you shall set in order your own house, for there are many things that are not right in your house" (D&C 93:42-43).

In the Book of Mormon we read King Benjamin's coun-sel: "Ye will not suffer your children that they go hungry, or naked; neither will ye suffer that they trans-gress the laws of God, and fight and quarrel one with another, and serve the devil." How many parents today are suffering their children to "go hungry" for spiritual food because they, the parents, do not have the Spirit of the Lord? Benjamin's counsel continues: "But ye will teach them to walk in the ways of truth and soberness; ye will teach them to love one another, and to serve one another" (Mosiah 4:14-15).

Dennis Rasmussen has written insightfully about agency and parental responsibility: "I can easily con-vince myself that I have no time to study scripture. But the truth remains: I do what I choose to do; I neglect what I choose to neglect.... If my children do not know the Ten Commandments or the Beatitudes of Christ, it is because I have chosen not to teach them. If they do not love the word of God, it is because I have not shown this love" (*The Lord's Question* [Provo, Utah: Keter Foundation, 1985]. p. 32).

Only through striving to keep the Lord's commandments and teaching our children to do likewise can we become what the Lord desires us to be—"the light of the world."

chapter three

He that keepeth his commandments receiveth
truth and light, until he is glorified in truth
and knoweth all things
— D&C 93:28

Achieving Your Divine Potential

We are God's children! Surely it is not unreasonable for a child to aspire to be like his Father. And since we have an Elder Brother who has succeeded in becoming like the Father and has received of his fulness, surely it is wisdom to follow his example that we might achieve the same fulness.

To do this we must trust implicitly in the Lord's counsel and guidelines. As we grow in light and truth, he will impart to us his divine power and infinite understanding. In order to achieve our own divine potential—our exaltation—we must do what he wants us to do and be what he wants us to be.

Jesus has expressly said to us, "What manner of men ought ye to *be? Verily I say unto you, *even as I am*" (3 Nephi 27:27; italics added). Through issuing this challenge, the Lord is encouraging us to develop our divine potential.

The Apostle Paul amplified this concept when he counseled: "Let this mind be in you, which was also in Christ Jesus: who, being in the form of God, thought it not robbery to be equal with God" (Philippians 2:5-6).

Since we are the spirit offspring of Deity, we should " hunger and thirst after righteousness" until these expressed potentialities become a living eternal reality.

Our Divine Lineage

To more fully appreciate our divine potential, it is important that we understand who we are and why we are here. The scriptures affirm that all of us are spirit children of our Heavenly Father. Elohim. The Lord assures us in one such passage: "I have said, Ye are gods; and all of you are children of the most High (Psalm 82:6; see also John 10:34).

The logic and beauty of this fundamental doctrine are expressed in the following poem:

> If God had not intended that I divine might be,
> Why then confer the image of divinity on me?
> Thus making my appearance a fundamental fraud,
> A being in his likeness, that never can be God!
> —*George Brimhall*

The human race thus has a far more favored lineage than most people perceive. We have *divine* potential because we are of *divine* lineage!

When we experience death, "the spirits of all men...are taken home to that God who gave them life" (Alma 40:11). How can they *return* unless they were with God previously?

Our Premortal Existence

Before coming to earth, all of us lived as spirits in the presence of our Heavenly Father. The scriptures refer to this as our "first estate" (see Abraham 3:22-26).

How long we remained in this first estate is not known; however, Brigham Young provided this inspired insight:

> I want to tell you, each and every one of you, that you are

well acquainted with God our heavenly Father, or the great Elohim. You are all well acquainted with Him, for there is not a soul of you but what has lived in His house and dwelt with Him year after year; and yet you are seeking to become acquainted with Him, when the fact is, you have merely forgotten what you did know....

There is not a person here today but what is a son or a daughter of that Being. In the spirit world their spirits were first begotten and brought forth, and they lived there with their parents for ages before they came here (*Journal of Discourses* 4:216).

Obviously, while in our first estate we learned much about the spirit world, its matter, its activities, its challenges. Evidently our obedience qualified us to enter what the scriptures call our "second estate." Those who chose not to follow God's plan—Lucifer and his followers—were cast out and were thus unable to progress further (see D&C 29:36-37).

The Second Estate

In order for us to progress in our efforts to become like our Father, we were required to enter a mortal probation. This next step in our education is meant to give us, among other things, a familiarity with the gross matter of our physical universe. This earth and our physical bodies have been provided to give us this added knowledge of the physical elements.

In addition, we are here to be proven. "We will prove them herewith," said the Lord, "to see if they will do all things whatsoever the Lord their God shall command them" (Abraham 3:25). Here in our second estate we are fully responsible for the choices we make and must accept the consequences of such choices. If we are in harmony with the eternal plan God outlined for us in our first estate, we may claim the promised blessings: "And they who keep their second estate shall have glory added upon their heads for ever and ever" (Abraham 3:26).

Our Noble Earthly Lineage

We have the potential to become what our Father and the Savior desire us to become not only because we are of divine lineage but also because we are the descendants of noble mortal progenitors. The first and greatest of these are, of course, Adam and Eve.

Discoursing on the greatness of father Adam, the Prophet Joseph Smith said:

> Commencing with Adam, who was the first man, who is spoken of in Daniel as being the "Ancient of Days," or in other words, the first and oldest of all, the great, grand progenitor of whom it is said in another place he is Michael, because he was the first and father of all, not only by progeny, but the first to hold the spiritual blessings, to whom was made known the plan of ordinances for the salvation of his posterity unto the end, and to whom Christ was first revealed, and through whom Christ has been revealed from heaven, and will continue to be revealed from henceforth. Adam holds the keys of the dispensation of the fulness of times; i.e., the dispensation of all the times have been and will be revealed through him from the beginning to Christ, and from Christ to the end of the dispensations that are to be revealed....
>
> God...set the ordinances to be the same forever and ever, and set Adam to watch over them, to reveal them from heaven to man, or to send angels to reveal them....
>
> These angels are under the direction of Michael or Adam, who acts under the direction of the Lord (*Teachings of the Prophet Joseph Smith*, pp. 167-68).

When we come to realize how greatly blessed we are to be spirit sons and daughters of God and mortal descendants of such honorable progenitors as Adam and Eve, we sense how far-reaching our possibilities for growth are, and we feel motivated to achieve our potential as we pass through this mortal probation.

I remember one fall season when, as I was walking through crunching autumn leaves and enjoying the beauty of the fall colors, I was filled with an overwhelming feeling of gratitude for the privilege of being on this beautiful earth and having a mortal body to help me enjoy it. I have had similar feelings while looking at cumulus clouds in the sky, or standing alone on a beach, watching the waves come in. Often, while looking at one of nature's panoramas, I have wondered how many other people have stood in the same spot and had like feelings.

Our bodies, with our five senses (seeing, hearing, smelling, tasting, and touching), are quite impressive aids to our enjoying this world of physical matter. It is a joy to walk in the rain, smelling the freshness of the air after a spring shower; to feel the smoothness of velvet; to look into the eyes of a laughing child.

Thus it seems that part of the purpose of our mortal sojourn is to learn to rejoice in the Lord's creations and in the privilege we have of coming to the earth to learn to become like him. Another important part of our mortal probation, especially as we seek to achieve our divine potential, is to be spiritually born again.

"Have Ye Spiritually Been Born of God?"

We need to know how to get the Spirit of the Lord into our lives and the liven of our families. We need to learn to recognize answers to our prayers. We need to know the feeling of closeness and comfort from the Lord. We need to pay attention to ideas that enter our minds, if the Spirit witnesses that they are good, and then act upon them. We need to hunger and thirst after righteousness. We need to choose to do the will of our Father in Heaven rather than our own.

To do this we need to be spiritually reborn. Unless this crucial aspect of mortality is accomplished in our lives, how can we lay claim to the promise that we will have "glory added upon [our] heads for ever and ever"?

In his October 1985 general conference address President Ezra Taft Benson declared the need for all to be spiritually born again:

> Besides the physical ordinance of baptism and the laying on of hands, one must be spiritually born again to gain exaltation and eternal life....
>
> The "change of heart" and "born again" processes are best described in the keystone of our religion, the Book of Mormon....
>
> Speaking frankly to the members of the Church, [Alma] declared, "I ask of you, my brethren of the church, have ye spiritually been born of God? Have ye received his image in your countenances? Have ye experienced this mighty change in your hearts?" (Alma 5:14)...
>
> Would not the progress of the Church increase dramatically today with an increasing number of those who are spiritually reborn? Can you imagine what would happen in our homes? Can you imagine what would happen with an increasing number of copies of the Book of Mormon in the hands of an increasing number of missionaries who know how to use it and who have been born of God?...
>
> The Lord works from the inside out. The world works from the outside in. The world would take people out of the slums. Christ takes the slums out of people, and then they take themselves out of the slums. The world would mold men by changing their environment. Christ changes men, who then change their environment (*Ensign*, November 1985, p. 6).

President Benson's emphasis on our being spiritually born again, in addition to our receiving the physical ordinances of baptism and the laying on of hands, introduces the must important element for bringing forth light and truth in our lives. Through our being spiritually born again, the Holy Ghost will lead us to all truth, "bring all things to [our] remembrance, and "shew [us] things to come" (see John 14:26; 16:13). Day by day he reveals to every person who has faith those things which are for that person's benefit.

Let us consider how this process of spiritual rebirth takes place. An examination of Jesus' words to Nicodemus can help us understand this important part of our Father's plan for our development.

Jesus said to Nicodemus, a ruler of the Jews: "Verily, verily, I say unto thee, Except a man be born again, he cannot see the kingdom of God" (John 3:3).

When Nicodemus then asked him how a man could be born again when he is old, Jesus answered: "Verily, verily, I say unto thee, Except a man be *born of water and of the spirit,* he cannot enter into the kingdom of God" (John 3:5; italics added).

Here we find then, two important keys relative to the process of being born again.

First, we must be "born of water." Of course, to enter mortality, we had to be born of water; that is how we emerged from our mother's womb. Every human being that enters mortality undergoes this experience. However, the Savior's statement above that we must be born of water has reference to the ordinance of baptism, by which we receive a remission of our sins and witness our willingness to be obedient to the Father. It is a symbol of our birth into a new life—a new spiritual life—and in submitting ourselves to this ordinance we are fulfilling the law. Even Jesus was required to fulfill this law, as he explained at his own baptism, "Thus it becometh us to fulfill all righteousness" (Matthew 3:15).

Second, we must be "born of the spirit." This refers to

31

our receiving the gift of the Holy Ghost and then, through our continued righteousness, enjoying his constant companionship. It is only by maintaining the influence of the Spirit in our lives that we can retain the blessings of being genuinely born again.

Blessings of Being Spiritually Reborn

When a person is born again of water and of the Spirit, that person "keepeth [or shields] himself, and that wicked one toucheth him not" (1 John 5:18). In addition he or she will:

- Experience a mighty change of heart (Alma 5:14).
- Be changed to a state of righteousness (Mosiah 27:25).
- Continue not in sin (JST, 1 John 3:9).
- Have self-control (1 John 5:18).
- Know God (1 John 4:7).
- Love the Lord and overcome the world by faith (1 John 5:4).
- Receive knowledge from God (Alma 36:5).
- Receive knowledge from angels (Alma 36:26).
- Receive knowledge from the Spirit of God (Alma 38:6).
- Taste of exceeding joy (Alma 36:24).
- Be filled with the Holy Ghost (Alma 36:24).
- Be sanctified from all sin (Moses 6:59).
- Be redeemed of God (Mosiah 27:25).
- Be quickened in the "inner man" (Moses 6:65).
- Receive the Lord's image in his or her countenance (Alma 5:14).
- Enjoy the words of eternal life in this world (Moses 6:59).
- Enjoy eternal life in the world to come (Moses 6:59).
- Achieve immortal glory (Moses 6:59).

Jesus said to us, "Come, follow me." When we do, we will be spiritually born of God and learn how to abide in Christ. Then will be fulfilled in our lives his divine promise that "if ye abide in me, and my words abide in you, ye shall ask what ye will, and it shall be done unto you." We may also qualify ourselves for an added promise: "If a man love me, he will keep my words: and my Father will love him, and we will come unto him, and make our abode with him" (John 15:7; 14:23).

The person who receives such blessings is truly born of the spirit, born of God, and is on the sure pathway that leads to a fulness of light and truth and the crowning glory of exaltation and eternal life.

"And Should We Die Before Our Journey's Through"

Another vital consideration in our upward reach and eternal progression pertains to those whose mortal lives have been shortened through what we consider to be untimely death. What about their opportunities to achieve their divine potential? Are these now forfeited?

Judging in terms of mortal timetables, we cannot give a satisfactory answer. From an eternal perspective, however, God's plan may be more far-reaching than many of us realize. For those who have lost young loved ones, section 137 of the Doctrine and Covenants provides hope and comfort. The Prophet Joseph Smith relates his experience:

> I saw...my brother Alvin, that has long since slept;
>
> And marveled how it was that he had obtained an inheritance in [the celestial] kingdom, seeing that he had departed this life before the Lord had set his hand to gather Israel the second time, and had not been baptized for the remission of sins.
>
> Thus came the voice of the Lord unto me, saying: All who have died without a knowledge of this gospel, who would have received it if they had been permitted to tarry, shall be heirs of the celestial kingdom of God;...
>
> For I, the Lord, will judge all men according to their works, according to the desire of their hearts (D&C 137:5-7, 9).

This vision received by the Prophet gives us the needed perspective to understand that the Lord does not deprive any of his children of the blessings of which they are worthy. Knowing this can help us endure patiently the trial of losing a loved one to what we consider an untimely death, a trial that might otherwise be heart-wrenching.

An example of such endurance through faith in God and his promises is found in the experience of one Idaho family.

At age fifteen Jared was an accomplished young man. He was a straight A student and a first place winner in the American Legion poster contest. He also happened to be a big fan of the Boston Celtics. But Jared's life was not to last very much longer: he was a victim of the disease known as cystic fibrosis.

Thanks to the responsive compassion of several people, arrangements were made for Jared to go to Boston with his family to watch his favorite team play. He not only watched them play but also got to meet all the players and take home an autographed basketball.

Three weeks later Jared died, just as his brother, Aaron, had died of the same disease about four years earlier.

In expression of their grief, as well as their supreme faith, Jared's parents had the following poem read at the funeral:

For All Parents

"I'll lend you for a little time a child of mine," He said,
"For you to love while he lives, and mourn when he is dead.
It may be six or seven years, or twenty-two or -three.
But will you, till I call him back, take care of him for me?
He'll bring his charms to gladden you, and should his stay be
    brief,
You'll have his lovely memories as solace for your grief.

I cannot promise he will stay, since all from earth return,
But there are lessons taught down there I want this child to
    learn.
I've looked the wide world over in my search for teachers true
And from the throngs that crowd life's lanes, I have selected
    you.
Now will you give him all your love, nor think the labor
    vain,
Nor hate me when I come to call to take him back again."
I fancied that I heard them say, "Dear Lord, thy will be done.
For all the joy thy child shall bring, the risk of grief we'll run.
We'll shelter him with tenderness, we'll love him while we
    may;
And for the happiness we've known, will ever grateful stay.
But should the angels call for him much sooner than we
    planned,
We'll brave the bitter grief that comes and try to understand."

Our Eternal Father does not forget his children. We should always have in mind his sacred promise as it relates to those who leave this life early, a promise that will give us hope and encouragement if we should ever have to face such a situation ourselves. He will provide every possible opportunity and blessing to enable his children—even if their mortal days are few—to achieve their divine potential.

Is It Really Possible?

Can we really achieve our divine potential? Is exaltation really a possibility for us? Sometimes we may feel that the answer to these questions is no. We are sometimes confronted with illnesses or problems that make us feel hopeless. Yet inwardly we realize that with God's help nothing is impossible! The secret is to trust in the Lord with all our hearts. If we will despise doubt and fear we shall rule over them on every occasion.

Doubt and fear do not come from God. In all our concerns let us acknowledge God and he will direct our paths and lead us to the solutions of our problems. In many instances God does not expect or desire us to handle our problems alone. He wants us to work in partnership and harmony with him.

Sometimes we may feel that gaining eternal life is just too difficult or that the realization of such an ideal is too far ahead in our future to think about seriously now. However, in our modern revelations received through the instrumentality of a prophet of God, we discover that some of our own progenitors have already achieved their exaltation. Examples of these great individuals include Abraham, Isaac, and Jacob (see D&C 132:29, 37).

How did they achieve this? The path they followed was, in essence, simple though not easy: they were obedient. When they were given a commandment, they carried it out without quibbling. They were dependable. They were stalwart, They were so faithful that everything they did was in obedience to the Lord's counsel.

Since these worthy progenitors of ours have already received their exaltation, let us see them as encouraging examples and take heart as we endeavor to progress in righteousness. Let us always do our best and pursue a course that will enable us to develop the same choice qualities our noble forebears had, that we might receive blessings similar to theirs.

Help in Achieving Our Divine Potential

Though at times the rigors of mortality may seem difficult and we may get discouraged, we can take comfort in knowing the Lord has not left us alone.

Elder John A. Widtsoe, in his book *A Rational Theology*,

clarified some of the conditions and safeguards the Lord has made available to us that can assist us in achieving our righteous goals. Following are some excerpts that I consider to be of great value.

> Man is not left to himself on the face of the earth. Though his memory of a former estate has been taken away, he does not drift unwatched and unassisted through the journey on earth. At the best, man is only a student who often needs the assistance of a teacher. It is indispensable, therefore, to know how communication may be established by man with intelligent beings wherever they may be.
>
> The first of the fundamental principles by the use of which man may confer with God is that man must show his desire to receive by asking for help. Whatever a man gains from higher surrounding wisdom is initiated either by a petition or by a receptive attitude which is equivalent to a request. Unless a man ask, he is in no condition to receive, and ordinarily nothing is given him,...To get help from without, a man must ask for it. That is the law.... It is probable that no request, addressed to a being of superior intelligence, is refused. However, the answer comes at a time and place not predetermined by man. Naturally, even though he asks, man has the right to reject whatever is offered him; in the midst of plenty he may refuse to eat.
>
> In answer to prayer, God may appear personally. There is no physical or spiritual reason why the Heavenly Father should not appear to his children in person whenever he so desires....To limit the powers of God, by saying that he cannot or will not now appear to man, is to make him a creature of less power than is possessed by man....
>
> Angels have frequently visited men and brought to them divine messages concerning their own affairs or the affairs of the world....These vivid personages, intelligent beings vastly superior to man, knowing well the laws of nature and therefore able to control them, may visit with man, though not seen with the natural eye....
>
> The chief agent employed by God to communicate his will to the universe is the holy spirit, which must not be con-

fused with the Holy Ghost, the personage who is the third member of the Godhead. The holy spirit permeates all the things of the universe, material and spiritual. By the holy spirit the will of God is radio-transmitted, broadcasted as it were. It forms what may be called the great system of communication among the intelligent beings of the universe....

By the holy spirit, which fills every person, man may obtain information from the Lord. By its means come the messages which transcend the ordinary methods of acquiring knowledge. By it man may readily communicate with God, or God with him....

In possession of the holy spirit is a record of the will of God with respect to all things and all occurrences in the universe, great or small, from the first day. The big problem of man is to read the message of the Lord as it is held by the holy spirit....

The giver and the receiver must be "tuned" alike, that is, must be in harmony, if the messages are to pass readily and understandingly from one to the other....

Prayer is the first and greatest means of reading God's messages, for by intense prayer man gradually places himself in tune with the infinite so far as his request is concerned.... A man should pray always; his heart should be full of prayer; he should walk in prayer. Answers will then be heard as God pleases. Seldom is a man greater than his private prayers....

A man must give himself to the matter devotedly desired in the form of prayer, and then support it with all his works.... Then, as a man devotes all of himself to the subject of the prayer, his attitude becomes such as to make him susceptible to the answer when it shall be sent. Prayer may be said to be the soul's whole desire....

Those who have given themselves with all their might to a certain study, often have great flashes of insight, whereby they leap, as it were, from knowledge to knowledge, until their progress becomes tremendously rapid, compared with that of ordinary men...

The gift of understanding or wisdom is the result of the

operation of the holy spirit. The help of the holy spirit, which is in communication with the whole universe, is available to those who give themselves devotedly and with all their heart to any righteous matter. It is one of the most precious of gifts, and one that should be sought after by all men, because by its aid the chance for development is greatly increased.

Literally, then, through the assistance of the mighty and all-pervading holy spirit, man is, indeed, always in the presence of God and his agencies. From this point of view man is always immersed in the light and power of Godliness. He, who by earnest prayer, close attention, and noble action seeks the intelligence above and about him is not alone. He walks hand in hand with unseen powerful intelligent beings and draws from them the strength that he does not of himself possess. In times of need such a man may reach into the black unknown and bring out hope, born of high knowledge. (*A Rational Theology*, 5th ea., rev. [Salt Lake City: Deseret Book Co., 1946], pp. 70-79.)

What a thrilling assurance! Thus in mortality we may enjoy any of several sources of spiritual help as we seek to achieve our divine potential. These might include the members of the Godhead; or messengers sent from the presence of Deity (angels, translated beings, resurrected beings); or the marvelous holy spirit, the light (power) that emanates from God and extends throughout the universe, as described by Elder Widtsoe.*

We should remember that as offspring of Deity, our own spirits can serve as open channels to the sources mentioned above. Our own spirits also serve as voices of conscience. Thus we have many marvelous resources given to us by our Heavenly Father that we might receive inspiration and guidance at all times.

* Note: the "holy spirit" as referredby Elder Widtsoe is often called the Light of Christ.

Let us never lose sight of the reality that Jesus Christ has a fulness of the Eternal Father's glory — light and truth. And he invites us to share his fulness as we are prepared to receive it.

We have, then, an open door before us and an invitation to enter in and receive all that he has if we will accept the invitation and continue faithful and worthy to receive the reward. It is as though Christ is saying to us. "All that the Father has he has shared with me. And all that I have I will share with you.

The Lord has given us another incentive and glorious promise as we seek to bring forth our light and become like him. We would do well to internalize this glorious promise "And if your eye be single to my glory' your whole bodies shall be filled with light, and there shall be no darkness in you; and that body which is filled with light comprehendeth all things. Therefore, sanctify yourselves that your minds become single to God, and the days will come that you shall see him; for he will unveil his face unto you, and it shall be in his own time, and in his own way, and according to his own will" (D&C 88:67-68).

chapter four

The spirit of man is the candle of the Lord.
— Proverbs 20:27

Becoming Channels of Glory

Man has infinite potential, but the only way he can ever achieve it is to *choose* to do so.

Dennis Rasmussen has written the following concerning our need to respond positively to the Lord " 'Wherefore, I the Lord ask you this question—unto what were ye ordained?' (D&C 50:13)....Man was ordained to disclose the divine; his work is to become like God....

"The Lord wants me, even me, to be his companion, 'Can two walk together, except they be agreed?' (Amos 3:3). As I hearken and obey, as I quickly respond, I show my desire to be in agreement with him" (*The Lord's Question,* pp. 6-7).

If we are to bring forth our light and thus become channels of glory for the Lord, we must actively pursue the indicated course. To enkindle the light in others we must first allow ourselves to be lit. My wife, June, has written about the process involved here:

The Candle

There is no light in a candle, unless it is lit.
Thus it can remain forever an unfulfilled possibility,
Unless it is lit.

For a candle to have its own light,
It must first make contact with a flame.
This contact must continue for however long it takes for the
    wick to ignite.

It may sputter, or melt too much wax, or refuse to burn,
But eventually, if the contact with living flame is held long
    enough,
It too will begin to "catch on."

After a short period of struggle
The new flame will burst forth and stabilize.
Now care must be exercised to keep it burning.
Candles can so easily be put out.

Now there are two flames.
The new one being equally as bright, and as strong,
As the one that helped it ignite.

Does it need the original help anymore?

No. A lighted candle can kindle other candles.
Now it can become the helper—for unlit candles.
We begin life like a bunch of unlit candles,
Waiting to be lit by someone who has succeeded in accom-
    plishing this in his own life.

So it is with man's spirit.
Unkindled it can be a dull affair.
But once kindled, it can illuminate a great future.

This is the power of Christ,
The same power—the same type or quality of power— Jesus
    Christ had within himself,
That is expanding—can expand—in each of us.

Thus can the Christ light—Christlike light—or power come
    forth in each man to envelop his soul.

An unlit candle cannot help light another.
Neither can an "unenlightened" man.

Jesus Christ is our exemplar.
He is our teacher, our guide.
He succeeded in doing in his life what we are trying to do in
    ours.

Reach up for the flame of his love
And remain in its embrace—like holding a candle
    to a flame—
Until you, too, have "caught" the flame of his love
And made it your own.

In a similar vein, my wife has used the metaphor of the
seed to explain our growth in spiritual things:

The Seed

A seed may remain dormant for years.
But its potential is still there—
Locked tightly within.

It takes the proper circumstances or environment for it to
    grow.
And even after it begins to grow,
It takes nurturing (sunshine, water—weeds kept away) for it
    to mature and fulfill its purpose in life.

So with man.
The seed of divinity within him will only begin to expand
    and grow into new life
When touched by the Spirit.
This contact must be held, continued—like with the candle—
For however long is necessary
For it to continue to grow.
The growing expands from *within.*

But just as a plant withers and dies from lack of water and
  sunshine,
Or is choked by the weeds,
So is man's burgeoning "new life" endangered by the wrong
  environment.

What is the wrong environment?
Negation.
It takes a positive atmosphere of love and harmony for the
  tender plant to mature and produce fruit
The fruits of the Spirit in our lives,

"But the fruit of the Spirit is love, joy, peace, longsuffering,
  gentleness, goodness, faith, meekness, temperance:
  against such there is no law" (Galatians 5:22-23).

Further explaining the application of these two metaphors, June has written:

Each of us has within us a seed of divinity from our
Heavenly Father. Like the wick of a candle clothed in wax, this
seed is buried deep in our subconscious, and may never be lit.

Jesus Christ also had a seed of divinity within himself. By
the time he came out of the wilderness after fasting for forty
days, he knew of his Godhood and had made the commitment to fulfill his mission in life.

He is a living example to us of how that seed of divinity
can grow and expand until it fills one's whole body, and
extends into the atmosphere beyond him.

That person who is following the Savior's example is "born
again," no longer swayed or enticed by the wiles of the adversary. The parts of him that were susceptible, his body and his
mind, have now been quickened by the Spirit to the point
where they no longer respond to the influence of the adversary, but are in complete harmony with the Lord's Spirit....

If you have felt the stirrings of the Spirit within you (like
the seed), try to have a proper environment for it to expand
and develop.

The key: positive thoughts and positive feelings—like
sunshine and water for the growing plant—will hasten the

day when you can receive the fruits of the Spirit in your daily living.

Thus will the seed that was implanted within your heart grow into everlasting life—for you! (June Andrew Babbel, *Onward and Upward* [Salt Lake City: Bookcraft, 1980] pp. 166-69).

Reach Up

As long as we are content to merely remain on our present plateau of learning and experience, we are not expanding our usefulness to the Lord. We need to continue growing. Rabindranath Tagore expressed this succinctly when he reminded us that "the dry river bed finds no thanks for its past."

God does not force us to grow in light and truth; rather, he gives us the opportunity to do so, and we, in turn, need to *reach up* for that additional light and truth.

Some people choose to define their lives according to goals achieved and missions accomplished, all of which they can check off as they complete them. For example, one person might say, "I have finished school." (Translation: "Therefore, I don't need to continue learning.") Another might say, "I've been on a mission." (Translation: "Therefore, I don't need to continue studying the scriptures or teaching the gospel—I've already done these things.") Other people feel that they have gone as far as they need to in their intellectual and spiritual pursuits, that they are already "authorities" and have no further need to learn from others.

Such people are shutting the door on their own spiritual advancement. How insightful is Andre Gide's reminder that "man cannot discover new oceans unless he has the courage to lose sight of the shore."

As we seek to bring forth our light and become channels of glory for the Lord, we should never be embarrassed or apologetic when we ask for help from another person, James told the meridian Saints: "Ye have not, because ye ask not" (James 4:2). Our willingness to ask for help from the Lord or from others is fundamental to our expanding our knowledge and experience.

We need to reach up for greater light and truth. Then we must stabilize it—like the candle—or embody it—like the seed—before we are ready to share it with others. The fruit cannot be picked before the growing is done!

How reassuring it is to know that we are not alone, that help, either from the Lord or from our fellowmen, is available when we need it, that there is always someone who cares enough for us to be willing to guide us on our way. Should the time ever arise that we become someone else's "welfare project," it may be a humbling experience, but we should accept graciously the help they offer and be grateful that they are willing to reach down to offer us the help we need.

This is the pathway to eternal progression—reaching up for greater knowledge and experience, and being willing to reach down to help those who may not be as far along as we are. We reach up to the Lord for his Spirit and his love, and with our cup running over we have plenty to share with others who might not be as blessed as we are. Some may not be ready to approach the Lord directly but may be willing to talk to or receive counsel and assistance from us.

Thus we can become channels in the hands of the Lord to help those around us—channels of glory!

This is what the Lord needs—people he can depend upon, people who will look to him for inspiration and then share it with others. Loving *and* serving: these are what Jesus exemplified when he was upon the earth. He was and is the perfect role model for all those who love him.

Reach Down

Just as there are those with greater knowledge and ability above us, there are those who do not have our degree of understanding or experience whom we can help. They need our support and encouragement, just as we may need it from someone who can perceive our needs. Among those we can help are our own children, our loved ones, and our friends.

Sometimes, however, helping others can be a tiring experience. Have you ever reached the point where you felt drained? Have you ever become so tired that you felt you had nothing more to give and you could not made up your mind whether to cry or yell or beat the wall?

Perhaps you have been giving and giving of your own spiritual energy without replenishing your own supply from the Spirit of the Lord. Instead of being a channel for his energy, you have been expending your own and have run out of it.

Think of holding a cup under a running tap until it is overflowing with water, with plenty to spare. Now think of a second cup that is full of water but gives and gives of itself until it is empty and there is nothing left. The usefulness of the second cup is limited by the amount of water it can hold at one time.

Often our attention is so much on the demands of each day—our work, our families, our bills, or the problems of others who look to us for help—that we may draw exclusively on our own strength until we are "empty."

How much better to be a channel (like the first cup) rather than a container (like the second cup). In this way we will not be depleting our own energy or power. When we become a channel for the Lord's light and truth, his Spirit will continue to flow through us in unlimited quantities.

Giving spiritually may be compared to the Savior's miracle of the loaves and fishes that continued to multiply, or to the widow's meal supply that never diminished in the days of Elijah: the more we give, the more we have available to give.

Each one of us has a unique role to play in making the world a better place. We have particular acquaintances and are in particular situations that could, should a crisis arise, require us to become channels for the Spirit of the Lord. We have the eyes and ears and hands that can be used for good, if we are willing.

Let us now consider a few experiences that illustrate the principles above.

She Was Not Afraid to Speak Up

One night after a basketball game, some Scouts who had played in the game were invited to the home of one of the boys to watch a video movie and have some refreshments. Upon gathering at the home, they noticed some R-rated movies sitting on a shelf and asked the boy's mother if they could watch one of these. She said, "Well, there is only one of your mothers that I know might not approve. I'll call her."

When she called, the other mother said, "My son doesn't need that." As a result the group watched something more wholesome. Thus, because that one mother was available when needed and was not afraid to speak up, the lives of a group of boys were influenced for good.

"I Would Rather Die!"

While serving as an assistant to the secretary of agriculture, I was directed to represent the secretary at a national conference, held in Gatlinburg, Tennessee, of the managers of the Rural Electric Administration. One of the managers picked me up at the airport and drove me in his car to the conference. Before he left, he loaded his car trunk with a liberal supply of alcoholic beverages for those attending the conference.

En route he drove me past the site where a new church edifice was being erected by The Church of Jesus Christ of Latter-day Saints. As we continued on our way, we became better acquainted and talked about some of my beliefs as a member of the Church.

After conducting at the conference my half-day session on developing effective management skills, I was invited to join all of those present for the reception in the beautiful lodge. I agreed to attend, informing them in advance that I would like to socialize among them but that I did not drink alcoholic beverages. They heartily agreed to have me attend just the same.

After the reception was well under way, I noticed that my friend who had brought me from the airport had apparently been drinking more liquor than he could comfortably handle. All at once he grabbed me by the throat and declared that he was going to force me to take a drink of liquor even if he had to break every tooth in my mouth.

I firmly told him that I would not take such a drink. I also thanked him for the kindness he had shown me in bringing me there. I assured him that if he resorted to such violence, I would be forced to resist, but that I would not do so out of anger, only out of self-protection. Then I said, "I would rather die than take a drink, and you know it!"

He seemed rather startled and then said, "You really mean that, don't you?" I replied that I did. Tears came to his eyes. He let his flask drop to the floor and pleaded for my forgiveness, which I readily gave him.

This experience reinforced my firm belief that no person needs to back down from a righteous conviction. The power of the Lord will sustain and defend such a person if his spirit is in harmony with the Spirit of the Lord. Moreover, we can gain the respect of those unfamiliar with our Church and our beliefs, and our example of devotion to principle may spark a nonmember's interest.

"I'll Be by on Sunday"

The father of a family of six children had an ingrained smoking habit that caused him to be delinquent in all of his Church activities and responsibilities. In addition, every time his home teacher arrived, this father managed to sneak out through the rear door of his home before he could be seen. However, the home teacher continued to be patient and persistent until one evening he happened to "catch" the father at home when he arrived.

After a brief visit, as the home teacher was leaving, he told the father that he would be by on Sunday to take him to priesthood meeting. After the home teacher left, the father told his family that he did not wish to go there smelling of smoke. So saying, he took all of his tobacco and threw it in the garbage can, never to go back to his habit again.

The sister who related this account in a stake conference ended her remarks by saying, "I know this to he true because that man was my father!"

If we persist in our attempts to help others, there is no telling how much good the Lord can bring to pass through our instrumentality.

By way of summary, President George Q. Cannon's counsel is most fitting as regards our need to choose to follow the gospel path, a path that will enable us to become channels of glory.

If you get to heaven,...if you sing the songs of the redeemed, you will do it, because you yourselves have chosen that path and have determined, by his aid. to walk therein all your days; if any are ever numbered with the damned, if any ever go into outer darkness and endure the misery of those who have rejected the truth and violated those laws which God has given, violated, in other words, the light that was within them, and which comes from God— if any be there it will be because they have chosen to walk in the path that leads in that direction, and Jesus came not to save them unless they seek to save themselves; it would be contrary to the plan of salvation if he were to do so (*Journal of Discourses* 22:242).

Let us choose to follow the Lord; let us choose to serve others; let us choose to bring forth our light!

chapter five

*We go to our death bearing in our hands
only that which we have given away.*
— Authorship unknown

Divine Love: Caring and Sharing

Although "we make a living" by what we get, we make a life by what we give. Therefore, the crucial measure in this life really is not what we get but what we give from within ourselves as we extend willingly and eagerly our love and help to God's children, our fellowmen.

As stated in a previous chapter, light and truth and intelligence are synonyms for the glory of God. Similarly, caring and sharing are closely related to divine love; they are divine love in action.

Basic Principles of Caring and Sharing

We need to share. But first we need to care. We would do well to consider the words of the Apostle Paul to the Corinthian Saints:

> Though I speak with the tongues of men and of angels, and have not charity, I am become as sounding brass, or a tinkling cymbal.
>
> And though I have the gift of prophecy, and understand all mysteries, and all knowledge; and though I have faith, so that I could remove mountains, and have not charity, I am nothing.

> And though I bestow all my goods to feed the poor, and though I give my body to be burned, and have not charity, it profiteth me nothing (1 Corinthians 13:1-3).

According to this statement, it appears that no amount of service to others will benefit us if we do not have charity as our basic motivation.

Another great crusader of righteousness, the prophet Mormon, clarified the true meaning of charity, bringing the entire matter into proper focus: "Cleave unto charity, which is the greatest of all, for all things must fail—but *charity is the pure love of Christ,* and it endureth forever.... Wherefore, my beloved brethren, pray unto the Father with all the energy of heart, that ye may be filled with this love...that we may be purified even as he is pure" (Moroni 7:46-48; italics added).

Jesus confirmed that the principle of love is embodied in the two great commandments: "Thou shalt love the Lord thy God with all thy heart, and with all thy soul, and with all thy mind. This is the first and great commandment. And the second is like unto it, Thou shalt love thy neighbour as thyself. On these two commandments hang all the law and the prophets" (Matthew 22:37-40).

When we truly love the Lord, we become channels through which his power and love can flow to other people. As we experience the Lord's love, we become eager to share it with others. By reaching out to them, we fulfill the second great commandment.

Forgiving and Being Forgiven

One of the most basic principles of caring and sharing is the willingness to forgive others. Forgiveness is one of the greatest manifestations of divine love and is a vital principle for us to understand and practice as we seek to bring forth our light through caring and sharing.

Our Eternal Father and his Son Jesus Christ are the perfect embodiment of love and compassion, which constitute the wellsprings of forgiveness. They forgive us because they love and understand us. This same love and compassion should prompt us to forgive others. When we are able to forgive someone who has wronged us, we can qualify to receive the assurance that God has forgiven us of the wrongs we have committed. As we sense this glorious relief, we are able to recognize and accept divine forgiveness, which transmits to us a marvelous sensation of an inner cleansing of the soul. Once we have felt this, the desire for righteousness will intensify in us.

In addition, as we forgive, we experience the joy of extending unconditional love. Such love constitutes the essence of caring for and sharing with others as God does. True righteousness flourishes in our lives when we exercise such love.

Nowhere is the application of this love more important than in our family relationships. Forgiving personal or imagined injustices within the family circle is essential to the well-being of every family. These grievances affect the lives of our companions as well as the lives of our children and other loved ones. Unless we rid ourselves of bitterness and resentments in such cases, we are implanting or justifying such discordant feelings and actions in the minds and hearts of all family members.

As soon as we become aware of any ill feelings we may have toward another family member, we need to act. Unless we quickly and sincerely plead for forgiveness for our ill feelings, we become Satan's emissaries and create a situation in which we may alienate ourselves and our loved ones from God's forgiveness. Such a course can only multiply misery and grief rather than invite harmony, love, and peace of mind.

If we become aware that another family member is harboring ill feelings against us, we would do well to ask forgiveness for whatever we have done, knowingly or unknowingly, to cause such feelings, Continued bitterness or resentment on the part of any family member is intolerable. We have to stop that cancer of spiritual darkness that will continue to erode our ability to care and share as well as our ability to feel the Spirit of the Lord within our homes.

The Lord has told us, "Of you it is required to forgive all men" (D&C 64:10). When we manifest unconditional love, we will forgive others and merit forgiveness ourselves. True righteousness becomes a natural byproduct. As this love continues to grow within us and we allow it to shed its light upon all who are near us, the light and truth of God will continue to expand in us until we have achieved our divine potential.

Following the Savior's Example

Our Lord and Savior has given us the greatest example of forgiving others as well as of every other principle of divine love. His atoning sacrifice revealed his infinite love for all of us and demonstrated what he meant when he said: "Greater love hath no man than this, that a man lay down his life for his friends" (John 15:13). Those who have a testimony of the truth know that the Savior's great act of love assures us of a resurrection and provides us with the opportunity to share eternal life with him and with our Heavenly Father. No one else has ever shown as great a love or made as great a sacrifice to make such an infinite gift available for all.

His is the example of love and gratitude we must follow as we seek to bring forth our light. If any person pursues his quest for light and truth in any spirit other than love and gratitude, his search may end up in bitter disappointment and misery. Genuine caring and sharing manifest divine love. Unless righteous motives and a spirit of love accompany whatever we share or give, such sharing may be a useless gesture. It "profiteth [us] nothing" (1 Corinthians 13:3).

Furthermore, if a person has been a recipient of light and truth and shares these grudgingly, if at all, not only will his action or lack of action avail him nothing, but also the light and truth he has may be removed from him because he has failed to share them for the purpose for which they were given him (see Matthew 25:29; D&C 60:2-3).

President Gordon B. Hinckley has reminded us of the importance of caring and sharing as the Savior did:

> Let us now in our time, each one, reach out more generously to love those around us in the spirit of the Christ. It is not enough even to give alms to those in need. For as important as that is, it is as Sir Launfal, worn and old, learned from Him who shared his crust, "the gift without the giver is bare; Who gives of himself with his elm feeds three—Himself, his hungering neighbor, and me" (James Russell Lowell, "The Vision of Sir Launfal," pt. 2, st. 8).
>
> May the real meaning of the gospel distill into our hearts that we may realize that our lives, given us by God our Father, are to be used in the service of others.
>
> If we will give such service, our days will be filled with joy and gladness. More important, they will be consecrated to our Lord and Savior, Jesus Christ, and to the blessing of all whose lives we touch (*Ensign*, March 1987, p. 5).

A true principle in every aspect of life is that we must give freely and generously because we wish to do so rather than because we feel we *must* or *ought* to. By actively giving of ourselves, we can make the world better for our having been here.

Rabindranath Tagore illustrated this principle of caring and sharing with a story that has strongly influenced my life, It reads as follows:

> I had gone a-begging from door to door in the village path, when thy golden chariot appeared in the distance like a gorgeous dream and I wondered who was this King of all kings!
>
> My hopes rose high and methought my evil days were at an end, and I stood waiting for alms to be given unasked and for wealth scattered on all sides in the dust.
>
> The chariot stopped where I stood. Thy glance fell on me and thou camest down with a smile. I felt that the luck of my life had come at last. Then of a sudden thou didst hold out thy right hand and say, 'What hast thou to give to me?'
>
> Ah, what a kingly jest was it to open thy palm to a beggar to beg! I was confused and stood undecided, and then from my wallet I slowly took out the least little grain of corn and gave it to thee.
>
> But how great my surprise when at the day's end I emptied my bag on the floor to find a least little grain of gold among the poor heap! I bitterly wept and wished that I had had the heart to give thee my all (From Gitanjali in *The Collected Poems and Plays of Rabindranath Tagore* [New York Macmillan, 1913], p. 19).

Caring and Sharing in Action

The following stories show the impact a caring, sharing attitude can have on the lives of others.

Paid by a Glass of Milk

Several years ago a physician vacationing in the Cumberland Mountains stopped at a cabin for a drink of water. A girl gave him a glass and then said, "Wouldn't you like to have a glass of milk?" The physician said he would, drank it, and then offered to pay for it.

The girl said, "No. We like to share."

Two years later this same girl was taken dangerously ill and went to Johns Hopkins Hospital for a very difficult operation.

The parents, who were poor, worried over the prospective bill. On leaving the hospital, the family was handed a doctor's bill for $450 marked, "Paid by a glass of milk."

Such are the blessings one who cares enough to share gladly might receive.

"Would Those Scouts Accept Me Now?"

While we lived in Oregon, I was assigned to a family as their home teacher. The father, whom I shall call Don, was a hardfisted lumberjack, a chain-smoker, and a liberal consumer of alcoholic beverages. When he was under the influence of alcohol, his temper would often flare up and he would beat his wife and children so severely that they were reluctant to appear at our church services.

When I first came to his home, Don refused to let me enter. I suggested visiting with him on the porch or out in the yard. At first he refused, but I persisted, and eventually we had brief talks together outside. When he was not at home I would meet with the rest of his family inside. Finally, one day he was there and invited me to come into their home.

During a later visit, I asked him if he had ever been a Boy Scout. I was pleased and surprised when he told me that he had been. He said that he felt this was a splendid program and that every boy should participate in it. He added that some of the things he had learned about the outdoors had been very useful in his occupation.

Then I felt impressed to say to him, "Don, we have a fine group of young boys at church of Scout age but no one to lead them and work with them. They really need a man like you who knows something about Scouting and its value. But even if you were the last man on earth, we couldn't afford to use you with these boys because of some of your personal habits which would set a bad example."

A couple of months later, he was home again when I visited the family. He told me that he had thought about what I had said to him. He had now given up his bad habits and was ready to take an active part in Church activities.

Then he asked, "Do you think those young boys would accept me now?"

He became a wonderful leader with those Scouts. His family grew up in the love of the Lord. His sons have been on missions for the Church. One of them visited us years later and presented us with an exquisite silver engravings he had made of the Washington Temple. Each time we look at this cherished gift, we recall the "mighty change" that the Lord wrought in the life of this father and the wonderful blessings which have followed.

I saw in my experience with Don and his family how caring begets caring, and I feel blessed to have been associated with these fine people.

The Best Investment I Ever Made

When I was eight years old the most meaningful mortal example in my life arrived in our community as a new convert from the Midwest. He was a letter carrier named Harold Chrisman Howell. He soon became known to us simply as H.C.

His one burning desire was to reach out to people and help them to develop their talents and to grow nobler in the process. I realize now that he epitomized genuine caring and sharing.

Since he owned a mimeograph machine, he volunteered to make available to all members in our stake a monthly mimeographed bulletin and letter combined with items of interest to increase people's faith, gratitude, and appreciation for life and the gospel of Jesus Christ.

I not only worked with him in producing this monthly stake paper but also soon became the assistant editor of what was known as the *Idaho Postman*—a newspaper designed for distribution to letter carriers throughout the state.

H.C. and I worked together several nights each week, which often resulted in my walking home during the wee hours of the morning. If I ever asked him about the spelling of a certain word, he would say, "Let's look it up," rather than tell me the answer. This developed in me a real desire for accuracy and excellence. When I asked about some gospel principle or concept, he would suggest where I could find the answer and would have me read it for myself. This developed in me a great love for all good books and a desire to gain a profound knowledge and appreciation of the gospel. Working with him without monetary reimbursement was the best investment I ever made!

H.C. also worked with others to form what was known as the Junior Genealogical Society, an organization for young people who were vitally interested in family history and genealogical research. Each year we went to the Logan Temple to perform vicarious baptisms for the dead. We worked on family histories as well as family genealogical records and had our own printed folders to incorporate our materials. We were encouraged to receive our patriarchal blessings and to begin living to make them become realities in our lives. We even put on programs to encourage temple activity. Our slogan was, "A temple in Idaho in ten years."

But this was not all. H.C. was heavily involved in Scouting also. His was a most fruitful imagination, always providing interest and learning for all of us. As a teacher of the gospel he was unmatched in his ability to create interest and a thirst for knowledge. He never seemed too busy to reach out a helping hand or to introduce a new and exciting idea or activity.

Later in life, H.C. was still dreaming up exciting and fulfilling activities for geriatrics and others. Organizing these activities has always been an act of voluntary service on his part, and he has filled several missionary assignments in the United States and Canada.

As I have traveled around, I have met many men and boys whose lives he has touched and influenced for good. I am grateful for his having shaped my life for good and guided me from errors. While I have met many people who reflect genuine caring and sharing, I have never known anyone to excel the beloved H.C.

"Speak to Us of Giving"

Perhaps one of the most beautifully expressed and forceful messages ever delivered outside of the holy scriptures on caring and sharing was penned by Kahlil Gibran. He enumerated different kinds of givers with their rewards and issued a challenge for more abundant giving.

> Then said a rich man, "Speak to us of Giving."
> And he answered:
> You give but little when you give of your possessions.
> It is when you give of yourself that you truly give...
>
> There are those who give little of the much which they have—and they give it for recognition and their hidden desire makes their gifts unwholesome.
>
> And there are those who have little and give it all.
>
> These are the believers in life and the bounty of life, and their coffer is never empty.
>
> There are those who give with joy, and that joy is their reward.

And there are those who give with pain, and that pain is their baptism.

And there are those who give and know not pain in giving, nor do they seek joy, nor give with mindfulness of virtue;

They give as in yonder valley the myrtle breathes its fragrance into space.

Through the hands of such as these God speaks, and from behind their eyes He smiles upon the earth.

It is well to give when asked! but it is better to give unasked, through understanding;

And to the open-handed the search for one who shall receive is joy greater than giving.

You often say, "I would give, but only to the deserving.

The trees in your orchard say not so, nor the flocks in your pasture.

They give that they may live, for to withhold is to perish.

Surely he who is worthy to receive his days and his nights, is worthy of all else from you.

And he who has deserved to drink from the ocean of life deserves to fill his cup from your little stream. (*The Prophet* [New York: Alfred A. Knopf, 1923], pp. 19-21.)

Wherever we live and wherever we go, we meet some people who are strong and others who are weak. Some are self-starters while others have weak "spiritual batteries."

Even as Jesus reminded us that the whole have no need of a physician but those that are sick, we should seek out those with real physical, spiritual, or emotional needs. They are on all sides, wherever we go (see Matthew 9:12).

But our first obligation is to strengthen ourselves. As we increasingly qualify ourselves to become channels for the power of the Lord, we can better look after those who are ailing, disconsolate, weak, or less active. This may include our own families and loved ones. Then we can extend ourselves to the best of our abilities, always relying on the Lord's help, to those around us. Then we can serve, lift, cheer, help, or strengthen our fellowmen.

What Should We Share?

What are some of the most vital things we should share?

Jesus said we should share the light we have received. In the meridian of time, when he spoke in the temple, he reminded his listeners "I am the light of the world he that followeth me shall not walk in darkness, but shall have the light of life" (John 8:12).

Later in his memorable Sermon on the Mount, Jesus challenged his followers: "Let your light so shine before men, that they may see your good works, and glorify your Father which is in heaven" (Matthew 5:16).

Here Jesus taught that we should share the light we have received in such a way that people, in seeing our good works, will glorify our Father—not us.

We should consider his message and challenge carefully. How can we glorify our Father in Heaven unless we are sharing his light and truth? Is it any wonder that we who have been invited to receive and share a fulness of light and truth—his glory—should be expected to be very circumspect and faithful in fulfilling the commandments the Lord has given us?

We can share the *light* (that is, the power of God working through us) by means such as:

prayer	father's blessings
testimony	our example
priesthood	
administrations	our positive qualities
temple service	love, kindness, forgiveness
wise counseling	service to Church, family, fellowmen

We can share *truth* through:

teaching moments	missionary work
counseling	business or profession
family	daily contacts

In addition we can share our time. We can share our resources. We can share our skills and talents. We can share our love. We can give of our time, energy, or talents without remuneration. We can give without being asked through our being understanding and perceptive regarding others' needs We can visit the sick, infirm, or prisoners, as well as our loved ones. We can engage in vital service projects for the benefit of family, Church, community, or nation.

Let us remember that genuine caring and sharing are manifestations of divine love. We should share because we care. Through our caring we make it possible for others to receive help from us without shame or embarrassment. As Gibran says, "It is when you give of yourself that you truly give," We may give of ourselves through a prayer, a smile, a song, a thought, a touch. But anything that comes truly from our hearts will have the power to touch the heart of another.

As we grow in knowledge and inspiration and recognize increasingly the power of God in our lives, we become stronger channels for good as we share with others. There is no limit to the amount of good we can do—if we don't care who gets the credit.

chapter six

*By this shall all men know that ye are my
disciples, if ye have love one to another.*
— John 13:35

First You Must Care

In 1950, while serving as management consultants to a
number of business and professional organizations, my
partner and I advised our clients to live by a simple maxim
which, when observed daily, achieved startling results. It
went like this: *People do not care how much you know, if they
do not know bow much you care.*

Observe that the caring comes first. Many of our
clients, including a medical association, reported this to be
the best counsel they had ever received and said it resulted
in great success for them. People are much more receptive
to counsel or help from someone who cares about them.

In order to truly care for another person, one must
focus one's attention on that person. This is what some
might term a "rifle approach," as opposed to a "shotgun
approach." In my experience, the rifle approach is the most
productive way to reach less active priesthood brethren. It
involves handling one person at a time. As my father used
to teach us, "He that chases two jackrabbits at the same
time will lose the one and not catch the other."

Years ago, recognizing the possibilities for success in

following these principles as a home teacher, I tried visiting only one family at a time (with the approval of the mission president and branch presidency concerned). What follows is an account of the results.

Bringing Back the One

In Oregon I was given the assignment in our small branch to be in charge of Melchizedek Priesthood activities. The only active members of this priesthood group were the three members of our branch presidency, the branch clerk, my business partner, and I—six in all. Upon examining the branch records, I discovered that a total of two dozen Melchizedek Priesthood brethren lived In the branch. In addition, about six dozen men either were completely without the priesthood, or, with few exceptions, were inactive in that priesthood,

I decided that my initial effort would be with those ordained to the Melchizedek Priesthood, After developing a plan, I presented it to the branch presidency and to our mission president for approval. They agreed to let us try it. This plan permitted the six active Melchizedek Priesthood holders, as home teachers, to give limited attention to the more active families assigned to them. Each was to concentrate his time and energy on one particular less active brother that he would select to reactivate.

Thus, to start, I asked each one of the other five active brethren to select one of the eighteen inactive Melchizedek Priesthood holders on our list. The job each of us had was to become acquainted with the *one man* each of us selected. "Become a genuine friend," I advised them. "Do this by borrowing a book, even if you already have it. Determine whether you have some books or tools or implements that you might consider sharing with the man you've chosen.

Engage in activities with him, such as golfing or fishing or other mutual interests, to establish a friendly relationship."

I further counseled my fellow home teachers: "You will be following the Savior's admonition, 'They that be whole need not a physician, but they that are sick.' Concentrate on this one man. If you have time, you may wish to call your other assigned home teaching families on the phone just to touch base, but don't try to teach them. Some among them may also be spiritually sick, but we will handle them later on the same basis until everyone is well."

All six of us accepted the challenge. Hoping to encourage the others in their efforts, I challenged myself to be the first person in our group to succeed. Each of the others agreed to bring his man back into activity within two months. At the end of this time we were blessed to see all six less active brethren reclaimed. Now we had twelve active Melchizedek Priesthood holders. For these twelve and their wives we had a special social during which the bonds of fellowship were strengthened further.

Our initial success sparked our interest in learning from the six who had joined us, as well as from each other, what particular approaches had proven to be most effective in accomplishing these results. I told them of the approach and follow-up I had used, as did the others. Prom these comments we began to glean some basic principles we would try to observe in our continuing Church activity. Moreover, these principles proved to be useful as we prepared for our next effort.

We also came to realize through this experience that each group that might undertake such a program would develop techniques based on the experiences of those involved. These might vary widely from group to group, as we discovered. We learned too, however, that those who become active are pleased to describe those actions which have been most effective with them.

Shortly after the social, the twelve of us were together, and I asked each one of the others to select one man on the remaining list of twelve. Once again each of us was to focus on a *single individual* and would not actively home teach any others, including any of our own twelve active families. This time we agreed upon a three-month deadline. At the end of that period twenty-four of us were active, and we held another social for ourselves and our wives.

One of the benefits our branch received from participating in this program was the great increase in love and brotherhood in the branch. In addition to his home teacher, each brother had at least one special, caring friend whom he had not known very well before.

Every brother holding the Melchizedek Priesthood was now active. This gave us twenty-four men ready to reclaim twenty-four of the remaining less active brethren. Meanwhile those in the branch who were not directly involved in the program were carrying on our regular home teaching activities. We were not depleting that group.

Our next effort, then, was with the brethren then classified as "Adult Aaronic" or non-holders of the priesthood. We followed the same pattern. Our mission president was delighted with the progress we were making.

Before the end of the first year, all six dozen of the remaining men were ordained and active. When I suggested to the mission president that we should request permission to organize two elders quorums in our branch, he was willing to have me write such a letter for his signature. I also mentioned to him that when the Brethren in Salt Lake City received this request, he would probably lose us from his mission since such a request would suggest that we should become a ward within a stake. Nevertheless, he signed the letter.

A few days later he received a letter from the First Presidency saying, essentially, "Hold everything." Two General Authorities were sent out. The Portland Stake was divided into three stakes. Our branch, now a ward, became part of the original Portland Stake.

This program worked in the mission field and it also has worked in a large ward.

The underlying reason for the success of this program is the recognition of the principle that "they that be whole need not a physician, but they that are sick! (Matthew 9:12). If each home teacher works with only one less active man at a time until he is successful, he spends his time where he is needed most. He focuses his attention on the one, and that one perceives that someone truly *cares* about him—and that love will bring him back.

Priesthood Power

The priesthood was given to man that he might fulfill the Lord's commission to his disciples: "He that believeth on me, the works that I do shall he do also" (John 14:12). Those who have been honored to receive as a stewardship the holy priesthood of God should magnify their divine privileges and exercise those priesthood powers right-eously forever. This involves genuine caring and sharing.

Many fail to recognize that the authority of the priest-hood and the power of the priesthood are separate elements. The Prophet Joseph Smith made the difference between the two clear on the great day of healing in Montrose, Iowa, when, as Parley P. Pratt later wrote, "he rebuked the Elders who would continue to lay hands on the sick from day to day without the power to heal them.

Said he: 'It is time that such things ended. *Let the Elders either obtain the power of God to heal the sick or let them cease to minister the forms without the power.'"* (*Autobiography of Parley P. Pratt* [Salt Lake City: Deseret Book Co., 1985], p. 254, italics in original.)

There is no power in our priesthood except through our personal righteousness. Unless we exercise the priesthood in accordance with the conditions God has prescribed—and this includes developing a loving, caring attitude—the powers of heaven are withdrawn.

The following scripture outlines those qualities we need to develop in order to exercise righteous priesthood power and to make our caring and sharing more truly reflect divine love.

The rights of the priesthood arc inseparably connected with the powers of heaven, and...the powers of heaven cannot be controlled nor handled only upon the principles of righteousness.

That they may be conferred upon us, it is true; but when we undertake to cover our sins, or to gratify our pride, our vain ambition, or to exercise control or dominion or compulsion upon the souls of the children of men, in any degree of unrighteousness, behold, the heavens withdraw themselves; the Spirit of the Lord is grieved; and when it is withdrawn, Amen to the priesthood or the authority of that man....

It is the nature and disposition of almost all men, as soon as they get a little authority, as they suppose, they will immediately begin to exercise unrighteous dominion....

No power or influence can or ought to be maintained by virtue of the priesthood, only by persuasion, by long-suffering, by gentleness and meekness, and by love unfeigned;

By kindness, and pure knowledge, which shall greatly enlarge the soul without hypocrisy, and without guile....

Let thy bowels also be full of charity towards all men, and to the household of faith, and let virtue garnish thy thoughts unceasingly; then shall thy confidence wax strong in the presence of God; and the doctrine of the priesthood shall distil upon thy soul as the dews from heaven.

The Holy Ghost shall be thy constant companion, and thy scepter an unchanging scepter of righteousness and truth; and thy dominion shall be an everlasting dominion, and without compulsory means it shall flow unto thee forever and ever (D&C 121:36-46).

Any time we are invited to share in God's glory—light and truth—the priesthood that allows us to do so can be effective and remain with us only upon the principles of righteousness, We must develop Godlike qualities, as mentioned in the above scripture, in order to do his will. When we violate the principles he has given us for exercising the priesthood, "Behold, the heavens withdraw themselves; the Spirit of the Lord is grieved; and when it is withdrawn, Amen to the priesthood or the authority of that man." Our honoring those principles will assure our being worthy instruments so that God's divine purposes can be realized in full. How sacred is his trust to us of his glory!

God gives light and truth to whomever he finds worthy of it. This is a privilege for every true believer. Those who receive the priesthood of God have a sacred obligation to magnify it. The responsibility of priesthood holders is to exemplify light and truth in their lives.

Bearers of the priesthood need to remember that they are examples to their families, whether they want to be or not. A three-year-old girl confided to me the other day, "My daddy yells at everybody." Perhaps cases like this caused the Apostle Paul to counsel the Ephesian Saints: "And, ye fathers, provoke not your children to wrath: but bring them up in the nurture and admonition of the Lord" (Ephesians 6:4). Should not this counsel apply to everyone who deals with children?

We Must Be Willing

To be channels for good in the hands of the Lord, we need to be a caring people. Both ends of the channel must be open if we would have the Spirit flow through us.

Thus it is that, first, we need to be willing to receive greater light and truth from the Lord or his servants. To do this we must be humble, aware of the magnitude of our lack of knowledge rather than impressed with the few grains we may have accumulated (see Luke 11:9-10).

Second, we need to be willing to share with those who need our help. If we are not willing to reach down to others, the time will come when our reaching up will be unanswered, and we will lose all that we have received.

People do not care bow much you know, if they do not know how much you care.

chapter seven

Whatsoever a man soweth,
that shall he also reap.
— Galatians 6:7

Making the Law of the Harvest Work for You

As children we may have seen fires put out by fire engines. We also probably saw mud cleaned off our shoes before we could go to Sunday School. But we most likely didn't realize that efforts had to be made to prevent future fires and to keep our Sunday shoes clean for Sunday use.

We saw these problems corrected and perhaps assumed that this would prevent any future trouble. But we know differently now. Until the *cause* of a fire is determined and checked, there is always the possibility of other fires being set from the same cause. Likewise we had to learn that playing in the mud while wearing Sunday shoes had undesirable effects and that we needed to change to play shoes for outdoor activities.

In other words, we had to learn what is commonly known as the Law of Cause and Effect. In the scriptures this law is known as the Law of the Harvest. Some people also refer to it as the Law of Action and Reaction. In any case it is simply the law by which we know that there is always a reason for a given condition or situation. There is always a cause for any particular effect we see around us. Each effect, in turn, becomes a cause for still another effect, and so on.

An understanding of this law and how it operates in our lives is fundamental to the development of that greater spirituality that will allow us to bring forth our light.

We Get Back What We Give

In the Book of Mormon the prophet Alma explained to his son Corianton the Law of Restoration, another name for the Law of the Harvest:

> Do not suppose...that ye shall be restored from sin to happiness....
>
> The meaning of the word restoration is to bring back again evil for evil, or carnal for carnal, or devilish for devilish—good for that which is good; righteous for that which is righteous; just for that which is just; merciful for that which is merciful....
>
> *For that which ye do send out will return to you again,* and be restored; therefore the word restoration more fully condemneth the sinner, and justifieth him not at all (Alma 41:10, 13, 15; italics added).

The economic statistician and business leader Roger Babson commented on this premise that one gets back what one gives:

> Briefly, this law is that for everything we do we get an equal reaction. If we boost others, others will boost us. If we knock others, others will knock us. If we help others, others will help us. If we abuse others, others will abuse us.
>
> As soon as I actually believed this law and began to practice it, my business began to improve. Since then we have continued to grow by making others grow, and have succeeded by helping others succeed. (As cited in Elmer Wheeler, *The Wealth Within You* [New York: Prentice Hall, 1955], p. 37.)

Such is the outcome when people understand and then intelligently apply this law. Nevertheless it seems that mankind spends countless hours and days, weeks and years, trying to overcome the *effects* of problems rather than eliminating the causes. Thus many of us invite the repetition of the same negative experiences in our lives, only perhaps in different settings. If we will learn lessons regarding the causes of our difficult times, we can avoid recurrences of the same problems.

Too often many of us increase our troubles by rehearsing them again and again to others and thinking, "Why do these things always happen to me?"

In addition we often observe people seeking "cures" for smoking, alcohol and drug abuse, unwanted pregnancies—the widespread effects of problems in our world. But who looks for the underlying *causes* of these problems? We must realize that if we do not identify and treat the real causes, these negative effects will be repeated, in one way or another, until we recognize the principle involved and take action accordingly.

Much energy is wasted by trying to alleviate the same problem over and over rather than using such energy to move forward. Instead of living for, say, ten years and growing in experience, many people feel they are on a treadmill, living one year with its problems repeated ten times.

These people are *victims* of the Law of Cause and Effect, or the Law of the Harvest.

But God did not put his children in a situation where they would be buffeted by immutable law. Man has agency. It was not intended that he become a victim of circumstances he could not control. But if we do not realize that we can change our situation, we become *victims* of the Law of Cause and Effect. In that case we become no better than the plants and animals, which have not been endowed with the ability to reason and choose.

Consider for a moment these familiar verses from the Doctrine and Covenants: "There is a law, irrevocably decreed in heaven before the foundations of this world, upon which all blessings are predicated—and when we obtain any blessing from God, it is by obedience to that law upon which it is predicated" (D&C 130:20-21). We might assume from this verse, probably correctly, that if we can find out which law governs which blessing, we can conform to a particular law and thus obtain the particular blessing associated with that law. Although there *are* many gospel laws, some with specific blessings attached, it is interesting to note here that the scripture says there is a law, one law, upon which all blessings are based or "predicated." Perhaps this refers, then, to the Law of the Harvest, a general law upon which it might be said that all blessings are predicated.

Here is a law, therefore, that can bring blessings. When we come to understand this law and apply it righteously in our lives, it will work *for* us instead of against us. With this understanding comes the ability to multiply the blessings in our lives, if we choose to do so. The Law of the Harvest is a law that can multiply our problems or increase our blessings since what we give we get back—multiplied!

The key to our benefiting from this law is our learning to employ those actions (or causes) that will bring about positive results (or effects). Once we realize the power and application of this principle in our lives, we can become the masters of it, using it to gain greater strength.

Thoughts and Feelings Determine Actions

In order to make our actions result in positive effects, we first need to focus on our thoughts and feelings. We should realize that our thoughts generate our feelings and our feelings prompt our actions. Thus *positive* thoughts will continue multiplying *positive* feelings and actions. *Negative* thoughts will continue multiplying *negative* feelings and actions, unless those negative thoughts are replaced by positive ones.

Furthermore we should know that it is impossible for a person to think or feel strongly without affecting those around him, his circumstances, and his own life. Whatever feelings you project to others will return to you, only with greater force.

Thus a person may multiply his troubles; by worrying he creates greater worries; by having fear he creates greater fears. Yet the same law may work to increase his blessings: by exercising faith he creates greater faith; by reaching out in love he creates greater love.

The harm comes when man, through his ignorance or stubbornness, becomes part of a chain reaction of negative feelings followed by negative actions. By accepting negative feelings and perhaps passing them on, he multiplies negative words and feelings, transmitting them still further to those around him. Such negativism can only result in negative actions on the part of many.

The person that propagates such a chain reaction is somewhat like an express train, running full speed ahead, with nobody at the controls to stop its devastation.

We truly are "our brothers' keepers," perhaps without our knowing it. The things we think and the things we feel are no less important than the things we say and do, since ultimately the former items determine the latter.

This dimension of the Law of the Harvest can be a source of righteous power to the one who uses his knowledge of it to multiply his and others' blessings. By controlling negative thoughts and accentuating positive ones, a person begins to limit his own negative actions as well as the negative *reactions* coming back to him from others. This is a "golden rule" for living an abundant life.

Once we understand that our agency applies to our thoughts and feelings, we will perceive that we can be in control of our lives. We will also come to realize that we will be held accountable for the thoughts, feelings, words, and actions we "send out" to others. These will return to us to either bless us or multiply our shame for our having disobeyed the counsel of God.

Guidelines to Make the Law Work for You

Following are some suggestions for making the Law of the Harvest a source of blessings in your life:

1. *Stop treating symptoms and start treating the disease.* Understand that, if you find yourself in a bleak situation, there was a cause that led to your present predicament. Realize that if you do not change your attitude (feelings) in some way, your situation may continue to become worse or more complicated. Do not spend endless hours trying to analyze and treat the various components of the problem; determine what caused it and focus your energy on that.

2. *Know that you can, little by little, remedy those things that cause problems in your life.* Try the Benjamin Franklin approach.

   Franklin listed the virtues he wanted to develop and worked on one a week, endeavoring to eliminate those things in his life that prevented him from achieving each virtue. When he had gone through the list, he started over again and worked at it until he felt satisfied with what he had achieved.

Likewise, when you identify something you do not want in your life, that has an undesirable effect, you should realize that you do not have to tolerate it; you can change it. Work on changing any negative feelings or attitudes you may have, and then watch how the Law of Cause and Effect will work to your benefit.

3. *Pray about your problems.* If you are uncertain about what has caused them, ask for help to identify the causes, then seek guidance for dealing with them. Follow the Savior's course: "I do nothing of myself; but as my Father hath taught me.... The Father hath not left me alone; for I do always those things that please him" (John 8:28-29).

Think and pray with all your heart, "Help me, Father!" Then follow the inspiration that will come. Condition yourself to pray first then act. Think in terms of *God's* solution to every problem.

Often many of us try to solve our problems ourselves, trying first one solution and then another, before asking for inspiration from our Heavenly Father. We may believe we should approach God only after we have done everything we can by ourselves rather than ask him for strength or inspiration or wisdom *first.* Although the Lord does expect us to "do many things of [our] own free will," we should realize that he is willing to provide guidance and inspiration that we might make wise choices and be successful in our righteous endeavors (see D&C 58:27; Alma 37:37).

4. *Know that the blessings you desire will also have causes that will bring them about.* Ask yourself, "What can I do to get the result I want? What actions will be necessary to achieve my objective?" Then, once you have remedied the causes of the negative situations in your life, use your energy not in looking back at those causes and their resultant problems but in looking forward to life as you want it to be. As you move ahead, you will perceive that the former negative situations no longer exist.

In doing this, note that you will have turned your attention away from the negative and toward the positive. Your changed attention will then become the stimulus—the cause—that can lead you to the effects you want in your life. Whatever we choose to focus our attention on will automatically multiply in our lives. If our attention is on our troubles or the injustices of the past, they will become our trials of the present also. If instead our minds are focused on the blessings we have received, or on love of God and family and fellowmen, these will grow stronger.

5. *Realize that the best way is the Savior's way.* His counsel, we might say, for making the Law of the Harvest work for us is that we love God and love our neighbors as ourselves. Wondrous are the blessings, or effects, that come from following this counsel.

As our hearts become changed and filled with compassion and love, our whole attitude toward people and events will change, enabling us to rid ourselves of negative attitudes and their negative effects. Our whole lives will take an upward turn. We will become happier, less judgmental, and more valuable as instruments of our Heavenly Father to bless the lives of our families and fellowmen. The law will be multiplying the good in our lives.

While touring Europe in 1937 President Heber J. Grant gave an example of a practical application of these principles. He was a guest at the German- Austrian mission headquarters in Berlin when I was secretary to the mission president. During a dinner there he shared the following experience.

When he and his sweetheart were preparing to be married, she suggested that after marriage each of them would probably notice habits or actions in the other that might be disturbing or annoying. She suggested that, since both of them believed in daily improvement, they should bring such items of annoying behavior to the attention of each other. In this way they might eliminate any problem of this nature before it became a cause of friction. President Grant readily consented.

Nearly every day after they were married, his wife discovered little things about President Grant that could be improved. As she brought these to his attention he agreed to work on them.

After several weeks she came to him and said, "Heber, we made this agreement before we were married. I have kept my part of the bargain, but you have never once found any fault with me. What is the matter?"

He replied: "My dear, you are perfect!" Then he told us, with a twinkle in his eyes, "And that is the last time she ever criticized me!"

President Grant's reply to his wife not only demonstrates that "a soft answer turneth away wrath" (Proverbs 15:1) but also shows how a generous and loving attitude is like a seed that, when planted, ultimately results in a bounteous harvest of blessings.

By increasing our love and understanding of other people, we can avoid emotional upsets and the adverse effects they generate. This is the Savior's way.

We live in a telestial world and are bombarded constantly with a barrage of negative thoughts and feelings from other people. Yet we know that Heavenly Father has given us the freedom to choose our own thoughts and feelings. It is our divine right. It is the principle that raises us above all other forms of life. Only man can choose his own way.

It is this freedom to choose that can allow us to benefit from the Law of the Harvest. Each one of us would do well to ask himself or herself these questions:

Is the Law of the Harvest working for me or against me in my life?

Am I a victim of this law, or am I a master of it, applying it in order to multiply blessings for myself and others?

chapter eight

Choose you this day whom ye will serve...but as for me and my house, we will serve the Lord.
— Joshua 24:15

Staying on the Lord's Side

As children we used to sing, as I remember, with great gusto:

Who's on the Lord's side? Who?
Now is the time to show.
We ask it fearlessly:
Who's on the Lord's side? Who?
(*Hymns*, no. 260.)

As adults we could well ask ourselves the same question periodically.

Having our feet firmly planted on the Lord's side is an essential requirement for bringing forth our light We always need to be close to the source of the light. In this chapter we will discuss what it means to be on the Lord's side and how we can *stay* there.

The Line

President George Albert Smith explained that there is a line dividing the Lord's side and the adversary's side: "My grandfather used to say to his family, 'There is a line of demarcation, well defined, between the Lord's territory and the devil's. If you will stay on the Lord's side of the line you will be under his influence and will have no desire to do wrong; but if you cross to the devil's side of the line one inch, you are in the tempter's power, and if he is successful, you will not be able to think or even reason properly, because you will have lost the Spirit of the Lord.'" *(Sharing the Gospel with Others* [Salt Lake City: Deseret Book Co., 1948], pp. 42-43.)

The words of the prophet Mormon help to amplify this concept of a "line of demarcation":

> All things which are good cometh of God; and that which is evil cometh of the devil....
>
> Wherefore, every thing which inviteth and enticeth to do good, and to love God, and to serve him, is inspired of God.
>
> Wherefore, take heed, my beloved brethren, that ye do not judge that which is evil to be of God, or that which is good and of God to be of the devil.
>
> For behold, my brethren, it is given unto you to judge, that ye may know good from evil; and the way to judge is as plain, that ye may know with a perfect knowledge, as the daylight is from the dark night (Moroni 7:12-15).

Clearly there is a line dividing the Lord's realm from the devil's, and thus there is a line of demarcation between the persuasion of the Lord and the enticements of the devil. There are two influences pulling at us here in mortality. It is impossible for us to respond to both of them at the same time. "A double minded man is unstable in all his ways" (James 1:8), Unfortunately, many of us vacillate from one to the other. sometimes many times in a single day. "Let not that man think that he shall receive any thing of the Lord" (James 17). We cannot have one foot on the Lord's side and the other on the adversary's.

Dennis Rasmussen expressed this principle succinctly: "The question addressed to man persists.... 'Where art thou?' (Genesis 3:9.)...Finally there are just two places, with him or without him, and just two ways, toward him or not toward him" *(The Lord's Question,* pp. 3-4).

Thus there are only two fundamental choices for mankind to make. Either we choose to serve the Lord or we choose to serve the devil. We need to understand what will result from our choosing one side as opposed to the other. And we need to understand that by our *not* choosing the Lord's side, automatically we are putting ourselves in a position where we are subject to the negative influences of the devil. Ultimately there is no neutrality.

The Devil Is Laughing

When we become too preoccupied with the daily, mundane activities of this world, we fail to be active, productive participants on the Lord's side of the line—a situation over which the adversary must gloat.

A woman of my acquaintance, Virginia Wheeler, told me of an experience she had that illustrates this principle. While in Seoul, Korea, visiting an ancient Buddhist temple, she saw a very large and impressive mural. At the bottom of this mural were the painted figures of several busy people, intensely engaged in their activities. Above them, apparently unnoticed by the majority of the figures below, were two scenes, one a heavenly scene and the other devilish. The figures in this latter scene, obviously devils, were in the attitude of laughing at the people below.

Sister Wheeler said there were two things that really remained in her mind concerning this mural. One was the look of rapture on the faces of the few people depicted in the painting who were turned toward the light of the heavenly scene and had made the effort to go toward it. The other was the look of glee on the faces of the devils, who were watching the majority of the people below. Not one of these people was looking upward.

The mural seemed to be showing that the people at the bottom of the mural were not necessarily wicked; rather, they were too busy with the many tasks and duties related to mortal life to have time or attention for anything else. The devils were laughing because these people, through their ignorance or lack of interest, had failed to realize that there was a higher way of life. Their apathy towards heavenly things made them vulnerable to the wiles of the devil.

God Is Light

Some people may object to the foregoing thoughts as they seem to suggest that ideas are either black or white, good or bad, from God or the devil. These people might point out that this is too simplistic, that in the "real world" there are all shades of gray in between. Perhaps, from our mortal perspective, this is true, but the revealed word seems to indicate that there isn't any gray on God's side of the line: "God is light, and *in him is no darkness at all.* If we say we have fellowship with him, and walk in darkness, we lie, and do not the truth: but if we walk in the light, as he is in the light, we have fellowship one with another" (1 John 1:5-7; italics added).

We might think of light and darkness (the Lord's side of the line and the devil's side) as being different frequencies. If we are "tuned in" to one frequency, we are *not* "tuned in" to the other one.

Thus it is that in mortality we have two opposing forces appealing to or enticing us. We can be "like a wave of the sea driven with the wind and tossed" (James 1:6), driven by the stresses and pressures of mortality, or we can make up our minds to live on the Lord's side of the line, where the Spirit of the Lord will comfort and guide us continually.

Thoughts and Feelings Can Keep Us on the Lord's Side

Just as our thoughts and feelings are the essential components in making the Law of the Harvest work for us (see previous chapter), they are the means by which we can stay on the Lord's side.

The scriptures clearly indicate that the Lord is interested in our thoughts: "Look unto me in every thought" (D&C 6:36); "Counsel with the Lord in all thy doings" (Alma 37:37); "Gird up the loins of your mind" (1 Peter 1:13); "Be not conformed to this world: but be ye transformed by the renewing of your mind, that ye may prove what is that good, and acceptable, and perfect, will of God" (Romans 12:2); "Sanctify yourselves that your minds become single to God, and the days will come that you shall see him" (D&C 88:68).

By concentrating our thoughts on the things of eternity we can keep ourselves in the Lord's territory. The Doctrine and Covenants makes our way plain: "Continue in patience until you are perfected. *Let not your minds turn back*" (D&C 67:13-14; italics added).

Perhaps more fundamentally, the Lord is interested in our hearts—our feelings: "I, the Lord, require the hearts of the children of men" (D&C 64:22); "The Lord looketh on the heart" (1 Samuel 16:7); "The Lord trieth the heart" (Proverbs 17:3); "The Lord pondereth the hearts" (Proverbs 21:2); "I the Lord search the heart" (Jeremiah 17:10); "Have ye experienced this mighty change in your hearts?" (Alma 5:14).

There are wonderful promises of the blessings we will

receive when our hearts—our feelings—are on the Lord's side of the line (see Psalm 119:2; 37:31; Mosiah 12:27; JST, 2 Corinthians 3:16; and JST, Romans 6:17-18). But to receive these we need to purify our hearts and remove sorrow from them (D&C 88:74; Ecclesiastes 11:10). We need to carry the law of God in our hearts (Psalm 40:8; 37:31). When we search for the Lord with our hearts, we will find him (see Jeremiah 29:13; Deuteronomy 4:29; Psalm 119:2).

Looking at the over five hundred scripture verses referring to the importance of our hearts (our feelings), we discover that God examines our hearts to determine whom we really serve. Hence we read in Paul's Epistle to the Hebrews "They do always err *in their heart*; and they have not known my ways" (Hebrews 3:10; italics added).

Why does the Lord seem so concerned about our thoughts and feelings? Because he knows that these can keep us either *on* his side or *away from* his side, depending on what our minds and hearts are focused on.

Our ability to maintain righteous thoughts and feelings and thus stay on the Lord's side is contingent upon our recognition that God works through positive feelings and the devil works through negative feelings.

The devil seeks to influence our behavior through thoughts and feelings. Elder John A. Widtsoe explained that "the devil, subject to God, is allowed to operate only within well-defined limits. He may suggest ways of iniquity, but he cannot force men to obey his evil designs" (*A Rational Theology*, p. 85). The devil has no power over us except as we permit it. We permit it through our lack of attention to God's priorities and our dwelling on or harboring negative feelings.

Following are some scriptures that describe qualities manifested or conditions present on the devil's side. These are the negative feelings that land us on and tie us to the adversary's turf.

Anger: "Fathers, provoke not your children to anger" (Colossians 3:21); "Satan putteth it into their hearts to anger" (D&C 63:28); "Satan stirreth them up continually to anger" (Moron) 9:3).

Contention: "Only by pride cometh contention" (Proverbs 13:10); "Satan cloth stir up the hearts...to contention" (D&C 10:63); "He that hath the spirit of contention is...of the devil" (3 Nephi 11:29).

Fear: "For God hath not given us the spirit of fear" (2 Timothy 1:7); "Ye endeavored to believe...but behold, ...there were fears in your hearts" (D&C 67:3); "The fearful, and unbelieving,...and murderers...shall have their part in...the second death" (Revelation 21:8).

The devil is pleased not only by our ignorance, lack of attention, and indifference, but also by our inability or reluctance to listen to and understand the answers to our prayers. Allowing ourselves to partake of the negative feelings mentioned above contributes a great deal to our lack of success in these spiritual matters.

This is not to say that the Lord *never* works through negative feelings. He sometimes does. But we may be assured that, when he does, it is always for the purpose of bringing about positive results. Thus if we are living righteously, striving to do God's will, the presence in our lives of what we may consider "negative" feelings may in reality be promptings from the Spirit of the Lord, urging us to take a particular action that will be for our good.

The following experience taught my wife and me that indeed the Lord can, when necessary, teach us with negative feelings.

We Must Change Our Plans

We were living in Virginia at the time and were planning a move to California to open a new business. We had done our "homework," knew the idea was sound, and intended to begin in Los Angeles, since we had been offered financing in that area. We were in the process of preparing our house for sale. My wife, June, tells the story:

"One Sunday night Fred went to church and I stayed home. I had an increasingly strong feeling that we should stay in the East and open up in that area. By the time Fred came home I was pacing the floor, tears running down my face (not normal behavior for me), and I greeted him with, 'You must call out West right this minute!' He did, and the decision was made that reversed all of our plans. We stayed in the East.

"We have thought of this often since that time and realize that, although we were praying about this decision, we had more or less accepted that a move would be necessary and were rushing forward in that direction."

My wife and I now appreciate the positive role that feelings of uneasiness, when prompted by the Spirit of the Lord, can play in our making important decisions.

We Do Not Have to Feel That Way

Negative feelings that originate on the adversary's side of the line tend to make us feel discouraged or even helpless. Such feelings can hinder our crossing over to the Lord's side. Therefore, we need to realize that we have the ability to change and direct our feelings as a part of our agency. We can choose our thoughts and feelings, but many of us do not realize that and consequently make no effort to change them.

When we are feeling confused or discouraged, it doesn't matter what we believe our problem to be—health, age, a relationship, education, or employment. Our *real* problem, more often than not, is that our feelings are negative, keeping us on the adversary's side of the line. We need to reach across to the Lord's side and begin developing positive thoughts and feelings.

Every blessing we may ever want—revelation, healing, comfort, peace of mind—comes from the Lord's side of the line. Confusion, worry, anxiety, and fear are from the adversary's side. We do not *have* to partake of these latter feelings. We do not *have* to feel that way!

At Christmastime we often read and hear a beautiful scripture, comforting words from the Savior: "Peace I leave with you, my peace I give unto you: not as the world giveth, give I unto you. Let not your heart be troubled, neither let it be afraid" (John 14:27). Note the wording of that gentle command, *"Let* not your heart be troubled..." It is as if he were saying, "Do not let your heart be troubled. You do not have to feel that way. Do not *permit* your heart to be troubled."

We often find ourselves in a negative environment. Many of our problems result from our absorbing these negative influences around us. Once we have "plugged in" to them, they keep multiplying and becoming more dominant in our lives. But we do not *have* to feel this way! We can replace these negative feelings with positive ones if we are willing to ask the Lord for help.

Our problems may seem insurmountable, but once we reach over to the positive side of the line, the nature of a problem and what we can do about it come into focus. An immense feeling of freedom and relief envelops us as we realize that we are no longer helpless.

How to Stay on the Lord's Side

To be happy in this life and throughout eternity, we must be on the Lord's side of the line and stay there. As we stay on the Lord's side for longer periods of time, we can receive, as we may need them, blessings of healing, inspiration, comfort, patience, and understanding. Cultivating positive feelings will help us deal positively with our problems; in fact, a problem may no longer *be* a problem for us if we have changed the way we feel about it. We can find joy and protection and peace of mind, in spite of a negative environment, when we have the influence of the Spirit of the Lord in our lives.

Such are the blessings of being on the Lord's side of the line. However, the challenge is *staying* on the Lord's side and not allowing ourselves to occasionally "slip" across to the other side. Let us consider some ways to help ourselves keep our feet firmly planted in the Lord's territory.

Study the Scriptures

There is probably no better therapy when one is trying to remain on the Lord's side of the line or to be receptive to healing or inspiration—than to spend time searching the scriptures.

May I suggest that, in your scripture study, you use a colored pencil to highlight scriptures and words of wisdom that lift your heart. You will be creating a collection of scriptures tailored to your own spirit. Then when you feel in need of guidance, inspiration, or comfort, you will be able to turn to those scriptures that will address your particular needs.

Some of the scriptures that I have found to be most helpful to me in my life are those that encourage one to stay on the Lord's side. Here are some examples: "Set your affection on things above, not on things on the earth" (Colossians 3:2); "No man can serve two masters" (Matthew 6:24); "Lay aside the things of this world, and seek for...a better" (D&C 25:10).

We can be strengthened further in our resolve to stay on the Lord's side by studying scriptures that describe qualities needed and conditions to be found on the Lord's side.

Faith: "Trust in the Lord with all thine heart" (Proverbs 3:5); "I will go and do the things which the Lord hath commanded" (1 Nephi 3:7); "Whatsoever thing ye shall ask the Father in my name, which is good, in faith believing that ye shall receive, behold, it shall be done unto you" (Moroni 7:26).

Love: "Love the Lord thy God with all thine heart" (Deuteronomy 6:5); "He that loveth his brother abideth in the light" (1 John 2:10); "No power or influence can or ought to be maintained by virtue of the priesthood, only by persuasion, by long-suffering, by gentleness and meekness, and by love unfeigned" (D&C 121:41).

Patience: "The trying of your faith worketh patience. But let patience have her perfect work, that ye may be perfect and entire" (James 1:3-4); "Continue in patience until ye are perfected" (D&C 67:13); "After much tribulation come the blessings" (D&C 58:4).

As we read about these qualities in the scriptures and seek to develop them in our own lives, we will inevitably maintain our position on the Lord's side.

Refocus Your Attention

Another way to stay on the Lord's side, especially if you feel that you are beginning to drift over to the other side, is to refocus your attention. Dwelling on stressful thoughts and feelings can pull us over to the adversary's side, but we can get back on the Lord's side by diverting our attention and refocusing it on something of a positive nature. This can be accomplished in one of several ways.

1. *Physical activity can refocus your attention.* In order to get your mind out of a negative mode of thought, you can walk, jog, wash the car, scrub a floor, exercise, clean the basement, or sing a song.

    One time my wife was driving five of our small grandchildren home from the doctor's office. They had all had shots and were crying at a fortissimo level, making it very difficult for my wife to concentrate on driving. She realized she would have to counter their noise with something of equal or greater intensity, so she began to sing in a loud voice, making up a dramatic opera-type story about children who went to the doctor. There was instant silence in the back seat of the car. The children's attention had been changed from being focused on their pain to being focused on the loud singing in the front seat.

2. *Mental activity can refocus your attention.* For generations people have read books, done handwork, memorized poetry, or held discussions to relieve stressful situations. These types of activities can also focus our attention on righteous thoughts and feelings, helping us to remain firmly positioned on the Lord's side.

    You have to experiment and find out what works for you. When you are feeling negative, that might be a good time to learn about something which would not ordinarily concern you, in order to control your thoughts. At least you will have stopped the negative feelings from multiplying until you can handle them better.

3. *Prayer can refocus your attention.* "Pray constantly," "Pray always," "Pray oft," say the scriptures. When the Lord said, "Watch and pray always, lest ye be tempted" (3 Nephi 18:15), he probably did not mean that we need to be on our knees constantly but rather that our hearts should always be filled with the spirit of prayer and thus

be receptive to the Spirit of the Lord. What better way to focus our attention and remain on the Lord's side?

Nephi gave us this priceless counsel: "Ye must not perform any thing unto the Lord save in the first place ye shall pray unto the Father in the name of Christ, that he will consecrate thy performance unto thee, that thy performance may be for the welfare of thy soul." (2 Nephi 32:9).

We should also know that, since effective prayer is two-way communication, we need to develop the spiritual skill of listening. Expressing gratitude to our Heavenly Father is also an important element of prayer and will help focus our attention on our blessings (see D&C 78:19).

4. *Looking for the blessing can refocus your attention.* Learning something from a seemingly adverse situation, something that can become a blessing in your life, is an effective way to refocus your attention.

Consider again the story in the Book of Mormon (see Alma 32) about the poor people who came to Alma for help. They had helped to build the synagogues and now, because of their poverty, had been cast out by the priests. They were greatly troubled because now they felt that they had no place to worship their God. "What shall we do?" one of them asked Alma.

Alma's reaction was not one of sympathy only, nor did he join them in their sorrow; rather he was filled with joy and immediately used this situation to refocus the people's attention on their blessings.

He told them it was fortunate that they had been cast out and thus forced to be humble, because in this way they could learn wisdom. "And now," Alma said, "because ye are compelled to be humble *blessed are ye*; for a man sometimes, if he is compelled to be humble, seeketh repentance; and now surely, whosoever repenteth shall find mercy; and he that findeth mercy and endureth to the end the same shall be saved" (Alma 32:13; italics added).

Alma then utilized this moment to teach them about the virtue of being humble "because of the word" rather than being compelled to be humble and proceeded to deliver one of the most beautiful discourses on "the word" and faith to be found in the scriptures.

Thus Alma helped these people, who had their attention focused on their poverty and their hurt feelings because they had been kept out of the synagogue, to refocus their attention on the blessings that could come from their seemingly adverse situation.

Seek the Lord's Help

The quickest and most effective way to gain strength and guidance for staying on the Lord's side is to ask the Lord for help. Some people think they shouldn't bother God with their troubles, especially when, as they suppose, so many other people with greater needs require his attention. But God wants us to ask for his aid: "Ye have not, because ye ask not" (James 4:2).

Reaching up to the Lord for help automatically puts one in a humble frame of mind, and humility is a prerequisite for receiving answers to our prayers (see D&C 112:10).

The Lord will not force our attention. He will not use a super sales technique to overcome our negative feelings. He will not violate our agency. We have to recognize our need and then ask for help. We have to want the contact with God in order to succeed. As we do so, we become enveloped by his Spirit. It is there all the time, but our negative feelings may be blocking our receptiveness to it.

The Lord explained the process we must follow to receive his help: "Draw near unto me and I will draw near unto you; *seek me diligently* and ye shall find me; ask, and ye shall receive; knock, and it shall be opened unto you"

(D&C 88:63 italics added). In other words, we need to draw near to him *first,* and *then* he will draw near to us.

So what should you say to the Lord? Just tell him how you feel. Remember he loves you. Tell him you don't want those negative feelings that draw you away from the Lord's side and seem unable to handle them alone. You need his help. Ask him to help you dissolve these feelings and to fill you with his Spirit. It is very important that, when you let go of those negative feelings, you ask also to be filled with the Spirit of the Lord. Don't leave an empty place for the negative doubts and fears to come back multiplied! (See Matthew 12:44-45; JST, Matthew 12:37-39.)

We may find added strength in praying with others for the Lord's help. However, we need to be aware that when we pray together, there must be harmony in our feelings if we want our prayers to be answered. If there is a lack of harmony in our feelings, and we agree that we need harmony, we can pray for that first.

The counsel of Peter to husbands is appropriate in this connection: "Ye husbands, dwell with them [your wives] according to knowledge, giving honour unto the wife...*that your prayers be not hindered"* (1 Peter 3:7; italics added). Though Peter spoke here of the relationship between husband and wife, his counsel can be applied to all relationships.

Once we bring ourselves to ask for the Lord's help to stay on his side' we need to learn to recognize inspiration. You might want to keep a pencil and a notebook handy to jot down ideas that come into your head day and night. Do not judge them at the time. The purpose of this practice is to help you recognize a new idea or an inspired thought when you receive it.

Remaining Steadfast

During a single day our feelings may oscillate between the Lord's side and the adversary's side of the line. But as we begin to take note of these fluctuations and make an effort to control them, we will find that our negative feelings decrease and we will be able to stay on the Lord's side of the line more consistently.

This takes practice! We must learn to identify negative thoughts and feelings before we can avoid or change them. It will not be long, however, before this becomes automatic, and we will be able to be cheerful, grateful, and humble much of the time.

It seems as though the Lord is pleading with us, "Come over to my side of the line. Here is the answer you are seeking. Here is the solution to your problem. You don't have to feel despondent. Let me help you!" (See Matthew 11:29-30; Colossians 3:2.)

When we "put on the armor of righteousness" and resolve to be firmly positioned on the Lord's side, we will be able to find joy, protection, and peace of mind in spite of our negative environment.

"We are made partakers of Christ," said Paul to the Hebrews, "if we hold the beginning of our confidence stedfast unto the end" (Hebrews 3:14). We need to gain experience in holding "stedfast" for longer and longer periods of time on the Lord's side of the line. Patience leads to perfection (see James 1 :3-4).

Paul informed the Philippians that steadfastness is one of the qualities needed to "be perfect" (Philippians 3:13-15; see also 1 Corinthians 15:58). The Lord has admonished us in modern revelation: "Stand ye in holy places, and be not moved, until the day of the Lord come" (D&C 87:8). If we remain steadfast, we can retain the remission of our sins (Mosiah 4:11-12; 5:15) and eventually obtain eternal life (2 Nephi 31:20).

If we will abide on the Lord's side of the line, we will receive blessings, and we will grow in light and truth. Conversely, if we allow ourselves to cross over to the devil's side of the line, confusion and darkness will increase in our lives until we have no light at all.

Our success in fulfilling the Lord's commission to be "the light of the world" will in large measure depend on our steadfastness in staying on the Lord's side. From this vantage point we can encourage others to come over and find peace on the Lord's side. Although some may not respond as we might hope, the spirit of goodwill that comes from us can permeate the atmosphere with love and light, which may eventually attract those who seem uninterested for the time being. We can dispel discord among those around us by living on the Lord's side ourselves, becoming conduits for the light of God to lift and guide others.

chapter nine

If you wish to go where God is,
you must be like God.
— Joseph Smith

The Joy of Abiding in Christ

Once we perceive the importance of staying on the Lord's side of the line and take the necessary steps to keep ourselves there, we are prepared to experience the joys awaiting those who abide in our Lord Jesus Christ.

Basically, *abide* means to commit oneself totally to complying with the mind and will of God. This cannot be accomplished until we have learned to establish an active two-way system of communication with Deity. Thus we may learn the divine will when we ask, "Lord, what would you have me do?" As we come to know his will, we can carry it out with his blessing and assistance.

The Lord made a significant promise to those who abide or continue in his word: "If ye continue in my word, then are ye my disciples indeed; and ye shall know the truth, and the truth shall make you free" (John 8:31-32).

Note that the truth which brings freedom is to be made known to or comprehended by only those who become true disciples. True disciples are disciplined followers. They become such by continuing and abiding in God's word. We must never lose sight of this prerequisite.

In two alternate translations of John 5:39-40 we find the Savior, in his rebuke of the Pharisees, stressing the importance of heeding the testimony of the scriptures concerning himself and of coming unto and abiding in him. The first reads: "You search the scriptures, Because you think by them to obtain [eternal] Life; and they are those testifying of me; and yet you are not willing to come to me that you may obtain Life" (Benjamin Wilson, trans., *The Emphatic Diaglott* [Brooklyn, New York: Watch Tower Bible and Tract Society, 1942]). Similarly the other reads: "You search the scriptures, because you imagine in them to have eternal life; and they are witnesses about me, yet you do not desire to come to me, so that you might have life" (Ferrer Fenton, trans., *The Holy Bible in Modern English* [New York: Oxford University Press, 1931]). These versions, along with the King James Version, imply that unless a person is willing, after searching the scriptures, to become a partner with Jesus Christ, his efforts toward salvation will be fruitless.

The Vine and the Branches

Let us ponder those poignant teachings and instructions Jesus gave to his chosen disciples regarding his being the "true vine":

I am the true vine, and my Father is the husbandman.

Every branch in me that beareth not fruit he taketh away: and every branch that beareth fruit, he purgeth it, that it may bring forth more fruit....

Abide in me, and I in you. As the branch cannot bear fruit of itself, except it abide in the vine; no more can ye, except ye abide in me.

I am the vine, *ye are the branches:* He that abideth in me, and I in him, the same bringeth forth much fruit: for without me ye can do nothing.

If a man abide not in me, he is cast forth as a branch, and is withered; and men gather them, and cast them into the fire, and they are burned,

If ye abide in me, and my words abide in you, ye shall ask what ye will, and it shall be done unto you (John 15:1-7; italics added).

While Jesus states that we can do nothing without him, he is also assuring us that if we abide in him, whatsoever we ask will be done.

What a marvelous invitation! Many of us have experienced many trying times and sometimes even seemingly insurmountable difficulties, and to abide in Jesus Christ is really the golden answer we have been seeking all along. How can we possibly ignore his plea? This becomes the key to all of our pure and righteous aspirations. To reject or ignore such a glorious partnership with our Savior and Redeemer in exchange for the alternative, an eternal life of misery, seems unthinkable!

Remember Your Source of Power

Once, as June and I drove our car into the parking lot near the mission home in Charlotte, North Carolina, we could not help noticing a wonderful tree. The bunk was very large—sturdy and strong and straight—with branches beginning high on the trunk and reaching up into the heavens.

A lovely little tree was growing out at an angle from the base of this massive tree. The smaller one had a trunk perhaps four inches in diameter but was about ten feet high with perfect proportions. The leaves were bright yellow, dancing in the breeze, nodding to us as if to say, "Look at me! Am I not pretty?"

We smiled at the delightful picture and at the winsomeness of the little tree compared to the strength of the large tree's trunk by its side. Then we looked down. Roots from the small tree were on top of the ground, encircling the large tree trunk as if they were hugging it, clinging to it for balance so the small tree would not tip over.

To us the tall, strong tree could have represented Christ, growing straight upward with no deviation. The small tree could represent one of us. It was free to "do its own thing"—to be beautiful, to put on its most enchanting colors, to dance in the breeze, so long as it did not lose its balance or forget its source of power. But that little tree *knew* what the source of its life and power was, and it was hanging on tightly to that source!

Our relationship to the Lord is much the same. He said, "I am the vine, ye are the branches...without me ye can do nothing." Yet *with him* there isn't anything that we cannot do as long as we remember our source of power.

Many problems arise when we think we ourselves are the vine—the source of life and power. But we are not the vine. This is the Lord's job description!

Neither are we the "fruit." The fruit is what we accomplish by being productive branches. "By their fruits ye shall know them" (Matthew 7:20). Our fruits are the results of our works, our goals, our aspirations. Whether the fruit is sweet or bitter will depend upon the source to which we looked for strength. If we are abiding in Christ, our fruit will be sweet indeed.

Thus we are the branches—channels through which can be brought forth good fruit. This is our job description, our responsibility, the reason we are here. We are to reach up to the Lord for greater light and truth—greater life, power, inspiration. Then we are to relay and share that strength with others in need who may lack the desire, the power, or the ability to reach up for themselves. We can meet these people on their own varying levels of understanding and then be prepared to give whatever kind of help may be required.

Considering this to be our responsibility, then, we might well ask ourselves questions such as this: Is the world a better place because of our presence? Do we try to lift up those around us or to tear them down?

We must understand that our earth was organized to help us learn and develop our abilities and to give us an opportunity to grow through service. The Lord has already learned these lessons. We must be willing to reach up to him for greater knowledge and then be willing to reach down and share it with others. But if we are not humble, our reaching up will be in vain, and if we do not reach down with love, our giving will not be acceptable to the Lord.

The vine has the power and the life, but it does not bear the fruit by itself. It allows the branches to do that, The branches need to be willing to draw on the power of the vine to develop the fruit. The branches cannot bear fruit by themselves either. As branches we have access to unlimited power as long as we remember our source of power and are willing to share it—like the example of the little tree next to the large one.

Jesus said, "Abide in me, and I in you." This does not mean that we should become carbon copies of him. It means that we should become friends and partners, sharing his love, power, and glory with others as he shares it with us. In such apprenticeship we may, in time or in eternity, be able to receive a fulness of glory as he did and become like him in word and deed. Thus may we achieve our divine potential and eternal joy.

To Abide Is to Be Faithful to the End

Our level of commitment to abide in Christ determines our eternal and everlasting joy or misery. If we endure to the end we can have "glory added upon [our] heads for ever and ever." Many may let this opportunity go by default, drifting along from day to day, simply because they have never seriously thought about it. They have never consciously made a choice and a firm commitment to abide in the Lord.

Others may have every intention of being good, honorable, and upright. However, as their lives become more complicated with family, work, and Church responsibilities, it becomes easy for them to neglect or lose their focus on the Lord as their source of power and divine inspiration.

As these people become more proficient in their professions and gain more experience, they tend to fall into the habit of using their own limited knowledge to make decisions rather than earnestly seeking the inspiration of the Lord.

Therefore, we would do well to assess the level of our commitment to Christ by asking ourselves questions like the following:

Are we truly Abiding in Christ?

Have we actually become his disciples?

Are we sharing our experiences and confirmation of victory with others so that we may retain the glorious blessings that result as we endure to the end?

These are challenging questions that we should strive to answer in the affirmative. No other alternative is worthy of any son or daughter of the Father, who so graciously grants us this sacred privilege of mortality and invites us to share with him even his fulness of light and truth, his glory.

Thus it is that to abide in Christ is to be faithful throughout our lives. The rewards of faithfulness are confirmed in the Lord's words to Joseph Smith: "You should have been faithful; and he [God] would have extended his arm and supported you against all the fiery darts of the adversary; and he would have been with you in every time of trouble" (D&C 3:8).

"Lord, You Can't Forsake Us Now!"

A wonderful example of faithfulness can be found in the life of Sister Anne Pienak, who lived in East Prussia during World War II. She lost her husband in the closing days of the war when the Russian troops broke through with their "scorched earth" method of advancing. She was left destitute with two small daughters.

During Elder Ezra Taft Benson's 1946 welfare mission to post-war Europe, on which I accompanied him as his secretary, Elder Benson and I visited with Sister Pienak and a small group of Church members in Selbongen (now Zelbak), Poland. While there we were denied permission to remove them as refugees to East or West Germany so that they might live among their own people.

Thirty-five years later, while completing some work in the Washington Temple, I observed that the shift supervisor was having some difficulty with a sister patron. When I inquired what the problem was, he explained that this sister had come from Dusseldorf, Germany, and since she could neither speak nor understand English they were unable to assist her properly. When he learned that I spoke German he invited me to help her.

She turned and saw me approaching. Then she exclaimed in her native tongue, "Oh! Brother Babbel!" It was Sister Pienak! I was amazed that she could recognize me after so many years.

I soon learned from her that she had come to the

United States to see her married daughter who was now living in Virginia. She then invited June and me to come to her daughter's home for a visit.

Later, upon entering the daughter's home, I noticed a large photograph hanging on the wall of the living room. It was a picture I had taken of Elder Benson with the Selbongen Saints. In the foreground was Sister Pienak with her two young daughters. That evening she told me the rest of her story.

During the period after the war, Sister Pienak's daughters reached marriageable age, and, being bound to the area in which they lived, the only young men with whom they might associate were Polish and Russian. These men were either Catholic or atheistic. Sister Pienak was distraught over the lack of favorable prospects for her daughters.

In the face of this crisis, she fell to her knees and poured out her grief and anxiety to the Lord. She reminded him that she had brought up her daughters in virtue and purity so that they would be worthy to be married in the temple of God to clean and worthy young men who would honor the holy Melchizedek Priesthood. Then she added, "Lord, after all the hell and agony we have gone through these many years, you can't forsake us now!"

Shortly thereafter she received a letter from the ruling magistrate giving her and her children permission to leave the Iron Curtain area to make their home in Dusseldorf, West Germany. They were overjoyed, for they felt that this was an answer to Sister Pienak's prayer.

After a short time a fine young recent convert from Romania arrived in Dusseldorf to get special training in computer science before leaving for the United States. He met the older daughter, fell in love with her, and they were married in the Swiss Temple.

Later a recent convert from Vienna, Austria, arrived in Dusseldorf, met the younger daughter, fell in love, and took her to the Swiss Temple to be married. The couple now lives in Vienna, Austria.

What glorious blessings came to them through their continued faithfulness and perseverance! The Lord did not forsake them. And, likewise, he will not forsake us!

When I later related this incident to President Benson, we both shed plentiful tears of gratitude. He had tried to get permission for this family to move in 1946. His failure to do so had always weighed heavily upon his heart.

Upon regaining his composure, he said, in effect: "This is a witness of the fact that the Lord's timetable isn't always our timetable. This good mother and her daughters had to remain in Selbongen until the time was ripe for her daughters to meet these two fine recent converts in Dusseldorf. Had they made a move when we felt it was urgent to get permission, this could never have happened. God truly works in mysterious ways, his wonders to perform."

What a priceless example Sister Pienak and her daughters were to me of how remaining steadfast in commitment to God can bring forth the blessings of heaven!

"None Shall Stay Them"

When we are truly converted and seek to always abide in Christ, we respond quickly to any requests made of us by the prophet and President of the Church. My father was one who was quick to respond, and through his faithfulness he overcame incredible obstacles.

In 1914 the First World War began. My father was serving as a missionary in Switzerland at the time. As an emigrant from Germany who had not lived in the United States long enough to become an American citizen before his mission call, he was faced with seemingly insurmountable obstacles to his returning home to the states.

He had been sent to Switzerland instead of his native East Prussia because Church leaders were concerned that, since he had not served in the German army before his emigration, he might be called into military service should war break out.

Several weeks before his call to serve a mission, he had been married in the Salt Lake Temple and, upon receiving the call, had to leave his sweetheart, who was expecting their first child. He had been in the mission field less than six months when his first son was born. Now that war had been declared, it was urgent that he return home as soon as possible to take care of his family in the years of crisis that the war would bring.

Unfortunately, when war was declared, the United States Congress immediately passed a law forbidding Germans who were not full citizens of the United States to enter or to return to the United States.

Knowing that these conditions existed, my father still made an effort to travel through France in the hope of at least reaching England. Three times he was arrested by the French as a suspected German spy. Three times the Lord inclined their hearts to release him. He finally reached England and made his way to the American Consulate in Liverpool.

When he discussed his situation with the consul general, he was told that under the law which had been passed, the consul was helpless to do anything for him. The consul general made it clear that, if he should violate that law by allowing my father to go to the United States, he would immediately be dismissed and be liable to a severe penalty and imprisonment.

Under these circumstances my father had only two

alternatives. He could either be imprisoned in England during the war or be returned to Germany, where he would likely be drawn into military service.

Realizing his helplessness, my father resorted to silent prayer. He simply asked our Eternal Father to keep his promise, made to his valiant servants, that "none shall stay them, for I the Lord have commanded them" (D&C 1:5).

The consul general, who realized the severe predicament my father was facing, apparently was filled with a powerful feeling of compassion for him. He assured my father he realized fully that his willingness to answer a call to missionary service under the circumstances he faced when the call came was an unselfish response which few people would consider making.

In view of this fact, the consul general was willing to prepare papers that would permit entry to the United States, provided that my father would agree to burn them and destroy the ashes as soon as possible after he had been cleared for entry. This commitment was kept, and my father's prayer was answered in what seemed to him a miraculous manner.

To me this has always been a firm testimony that when a person is on the Lord's side of the line, abiding in Christ, God will never forsake him. And I feel that in my lifetime he never has forsaken me!

Preparing to Perform the "Greater Works"

As we continue to abide in Christ, we should examine and ponder the significance of Jesus' words to his Apostles—or his "friends," as he called them "Verily, verily I say unto you. He that believeth on me, the works that I do shall he do also; and greater works than these shall he do; because I go unto my Father. And whatsoever ye shall ask in my name, that will I do, that the Father may be glorified in the Son. If ye shall ask any thing in my name, I will do it" (John 14:12-14).

Interpreting these verses, Joseph Smith taught that "the greater works which those that believed on his name were to do were to be done in eternity, where he was going and where they should behold his glory" *(Lectures on Faith* 7:12). This statement helps us to envision the great opportunities that await us in eternity if we humbly prepare for them now by being faithful and abiding in Christ.

Nevertheless the Lord has also provided us with opportunities to perform great works in this life. Consider, for instance, the responsibility and blessing we have been given to perform vicarious temple ordinances for the dead. This monumental opportunity has been made possible by the Savior's visit to the spirit world between the time of his crucifixion and resurrection. There he organized a missionary force among the righteous spirits that would go to preach to those who had died without accepting or without hearing the gospel message. The ordinances of salvation would then need to be performed by those on earth in behalf of these departed spirits.

Thus Christ has opened the door to this glorious work for the dead, but he relies on faithful Latter-day Saints to enter the temples and perform the vicarious ordinances for those on the other side of the veil. It is in this way that we truly become "saviors on Mount Zion" (see Obadiah 1:21; D&C 103:9-10). Given these circumstances, we can begin to appreciate the tremendous opportunity offered us to officiate for the dead in the temples, assisting the Lord in his work "to bring to pass the immortality and eternal life of man" (Moses 1:39). Indeed we might even think of this work for the dead as one of the "greater works" mentioned by the Savior, at least in the sense that this is a work he could not perform personally; our willing cooperation and service are needed.

There is really nothing more important, more faith-promoting, or more crucial to our own and others, salvation than serving in the temples. Besides facilitating the development within us of such divine attributes as obedience and charity, the active and intensive service we render in this life in the temples will have far-reaching effects throughout the eternities, affording ourselves and others blessings beyond what we can possibly imagine. The Prophet Joseph Smith understood the magnitude of this great work and its attendant blessings. "Concerning the work for the dead," Horace Cummings reported, "he [Joseph Smith] said that in the resurrection those who had been worked for would fall at the feet of those who had done their work, kiss their feet, embrace their knees and manifest the most exquisite gratitude." The Prophet continued, "We do not comprehend what a blessing to them these ordinances are." (As cited in N. B. Lundwall, comp., *The Vision* [Salt Lake City: Bookcraft, n.d.], p. 141.) Thus, as we anticipate and prepare for the "greater works" to be performed in eternity, let us not lose sight of the eternal value of the great things we can achieve here in mortality.

In addition, we need to realize that the "greater works" are to be accomplished only by those who truly believe, who faithfully abide in Christ. What does it mean to truly believe? It means to be as Jesus is and to live as Jesus lived while in his mortal ministry—to be channels of glory in his hands.

Elder Melvin J. Ballard of the Quorum of the Twelve Apostles used to delight audiences by singing, in his melodious voice, his favorite song: "I'll go where you want me to go.... I'll say what you want me to say.... I'll do thy will with a heart sincere: I'll be what you want me to be" *(Hymns,* no. 270). The words of this hymn embody the Lord's desire that we should be even as he is and live as he lived. Keeping the commandments of God and growing in light and truth will enable us to achieve what he asked us to achieve because we too are offspring of Deity. We would do well to read the words of this hymn, "I'll Go Where You Want Me to Go," and sing it with such feeling that we may internalize its message.

Our Challenge

What then is our challenge? First, to find a quiet place and a quiet moment alone to stop—stop and be still. Second, to examine our hearts. Do we love the Lord? Do we realize his great love for us? Do we often feel the sweet comfort of his Spirit or the thrilling enlightenment of his inspiration?

Each one of us should ask him or herself:

What do I want to be like twenty years from now?

Am I on the right road, going in the right direction *now?*

Am I moving (growing spiritually) *now?*

Is it the desire of my heart to do the will of the Lord *now?*

What can I do to strengthen my bond with the Lord so that I could walk by his side without feeling uncomfortable?

We must be even as Jesus is; we must live even as Jesus lived; we must do as Jesus did—loving and teaching, caring and serving. As we do this, we will experience the joys of abiding in Christ.

In addition, we need to realize that it is only through his power or light that we can participate in his work of bringing to pass the eternal life of God's children And even as we reach out to others, he will be reaching out to us.

Jesus said that "the Son can do nothing of himself, but what he seeth the Father do" (John 5:19). And later he stated,

"The Father that dwelleth in me, he doeth the works" (John 14:10). If this is true of Christ, how can any mere mortal think that he has the power to do the works of Christ unless he abides in the vine? He should live in harmony with that "still small voice" of God centered in his own soul. He must develop his ears to hear the whisperings of the Spirit.

When a person abides in Christ, his soul is filled with light and no darkness can enter in. He who has learned to "be still and know" that the Lord is God has opened the door, and Christ no longer needs to stand without, knocking, but can enter and sup with him. Such a person's inner being becomes a temple, within which he will be protected from the darkness and confusion of the world.

chapter ten

What manner of men ought ye to be?
Verily I say unto you, even as I am.
— 3 Nephi 27:27

"Teach Me All That I Must Be"

We were commanded by the Lord to be the light of the world, to be the salt of the earth. Jesus further challenged us "Let your light so shine before men, that they may see your good works, and glorify your Father which is in Heaven" (Matthew 5:16).

To fulfill these admonitions, we must radiate light and truth to others. We are to be "the leaven" among the people (see Matthew 13:33). Many of our fellowmen and women need living examples that manifest the fruits of righteousness. If it is true that "by their fruits ye shall know them," that fruit must be brought forth by those who are committed to a righteous way of life.

We need to manifest our love and commitment to God by being like our Lord and Savior, by doing what is right in the sight of God, and by living our lives in accordance with divine principles, In this manner the testing and probation of our earth life will result in our bringing forth those qualities that will qualify us to abide in his presence, as we did before we accepted this wonderful mortal opportunity.

Hence, it is not sufficient for us to only *know* and *do* the will of God; we also need to *be*, to *become*, like the Lord. "What manner of men ought ye to be? Verily I say unto you, even as I am" (3 Nephi 27:27).

The divine commandment we have received to bring up our children in light and truth requires us, essentially, to be and live as examples of the qualities that radiate from a celestial pattern of thought and living. Children who are brought up in such an atmosphere will avoid any adverse enticement because they will have been brought up in light, and any darkness will be abhorrent to them. The devil began his campaign to dominate the minds and hearts of men with Adam's children. He is increasing his pressure on our children and us in our day. However, as our children are brought up in the very living presence of light and truth, they will likewise exert every effort to achieve and maintain the same light and truth in their lives.

The Lord wants us to be like him and to live in accordance with divine principles as he himself does. When we commit ourselves to establishing and maintaining this pattern, he will abide in us and will lead us by the hand. "And ye shall seek me, and find me, when ye shall search for me with all your heart" (Jeremiah 29:13).

To succeed we should, above all else, open our hearts to the Spirit of the Lord. In this way we may reflect every divine feeling of love, compassion, forgiveness, patience, and selflessness. In addition, we must also maintain humble and teachable spirits, hungering and thirsting for light and truth.

This must become a total way of life. Then we will receive grace for grace, even as Jesus did, until we enjoy even that fulness that he has promised we can achieve. In that promise is reflected his total unselfishness and his grand design that we become like him in every divine feeling and thought.

We cannot share the light until we ourselves possess it. Then, as we bring forth our light, we need to remember that actions speak louder than words How true is the adage, "Your actions speak so loudly that I cannot hear what you say"!

In the Book of Mormon the series of questions that Alma asks members of the Church indicate at least three primary qualities we all should develop if we would he a light to others (see Alma 5), Let us review three specific questions from Alma 5:14 that highlight these qualities:

1. *"Have ye spiritually been born of God?"* No person has achieved this unless he is living a Spirit-directed life and is manifesting the fruits of true spirituality. Having hands laid upon our heads and hearing the admonition, "Receive the Holy Ghost," is only the invitation to open our lives to such divine direction and companionship. Unless we have truly sought for and received the companionship of the Holy Ghost in our lives, we have not been spiritually born of God as our living prophet, President Benson, has challenged us to be.

2. *"Have ye received his image in your countenances?"* This is the image that radiates light and truth—the glory of God. As the Savior manifested such light during his mortal ministry, the honest in heart were drawn to him. This same quality will draw to us our children, our families, and all those whose lives we touch.

3. *"Have ye experienced this mighty change in your hearts?"* If we don't know exactly what this means, then we haven't experienced it. This is the mighty change that literally lifts us from living and feeling and thinking on a mortal, worldly level to living and abiding on an entirely spiritual level.

When we can answer these questions in the affirmative, we are well on our way to becoming the "light of the world.

" Unfortunately, it seems that many people place so much stress upon observing "the letter of the law" that these divine qualities are rarely understood or sought after in their lives.

In our day a beautiful song has become a joyous classic with young and old alike: "I Am a Child of God" *(Hymns,* no 301). Originally this song concluded with "Teach me all that I must *know* to live with him someday." President Spencer W. Kimball suggested that this should be changed to "Teach me all that I must *do...*" This change emphasized the need for us nor only to know the Father's will but also to do it.

In view of what the Lord truly desires us to become that we might be able to meet the challenges facing us today, we might ponder another change in the song's lyrics, as pointed out by Susan Easton Black. Perhaps we could sing: "Teach me all that must *be...*" (see *Finding Christ Through the Book of Mormon* [Deseret Book Co., 1987], p. 50).

The great invitation extended to us to work with the Lord in bringing about our divine potential is often all but completely bypassed because of other demands upon our time and attention. However, if we will accept the invitation and commit ourselves to manifest the fruits of light and truth by being and living in accordance with God's celestial principles, we shall be victorious. Light (the power of God) and truth (the knowledge from God) will thus be exemplified in our lives.

We must be products of celestial laws applied unceasingly to our lives if we are to inherit the celestial kingdom of God. Through outward ordinances we receive the invitation and promise that "through our faithfulness" we will obtain the blessings we seek. The word *faithfulness* suggests a fulness of faith applied to our efforts to become that which we have been invited and challenged to become. If we truly are celestial beings in embryo, we have every valid reason to become what our divine Father desires us to be' even as he and our Lord are (see 3 Nephi 12:4).

In October 1988 general conference our modern-day prophet, Ezra Taft Benson, spoke as directly and plainly as can be. He said "God's wrath will soon shake the nations of the earth and will be poured out on the wicked without measure...I testify that it is time for every man to set in order his own house both temporally and spiritually.... It is time for us, as members of the Church, to walk in all the ways of the Lord, to use our influence to make popular that which is sound and to make unpopular that which is unsound.... Now we need eyes that will see, ears that will hear, and hearts that will hearken to God's direction. I testify that not many years hence the earth will be cleansed" (*Ensign,* November 1988, p. 87).

The time is short. It is urgent that we prepare ourselves for that great day when our Lord will return.

Let us resolve to accept the Lord's invitation and work with him to bring about the eternal life of ourselves and others, which he cannot do without our daily participation. Let us truly be the "light of the world. "

We must know.
We must do.
We must be.

Bring forth your light!

Index

126

J

Jacob (Old Testament prophet), 36
James, on asking, 44
  on drawing nigh to God, 14
  on patience, 20
Jesus Christ, 28, 63, 69-70, 61
  abiding in, 9, 103-117
  atonement of, 10, 56
  baptism, 31
  change through, 31
  commitment to, 106
  disciples of, 103-104
  example of, 4, 11, 24, 44, 45, 56, 107
  fulness received by, 10, 18, 24, 39, 120
  image in countenances, 121
  light of, 39, 53
  light of the world, *vii*, 3, 23, 64
  love of, 54
  miracle of the loaves and fishes, 48
  missionary work in spirit world, 114
  on being born of water and of the spirit, 30
  on greater works, 113-115
  on letting light shine, 119
  on love, 52
  on peace, 91
  parable of the wise and foolish virgins, 13
  power of, 38, 42
  relationship with, 106
  resurrection, 10
  second coming of, 123
  Sermon on the Mount, *64*
  teachings, 3
  true vine, 104
  truth shared by, 3-4
  See also God
John the Apostle, on being like God, 8
John the Baptist, on Christ, 10
Johns Hopkins Hospital, 59
Journal of Discourses, 6, 18, 26, 50
Joy, 7, 9, 29, 55, 62-63, 94, 96, 100, 102, 107
Junior Genealogical Society, 60

K

Kimball, Heber C., on borrowed light, 13-14
Kindness, 64
Knowledge, 4-7, 32, 38, 46, 61, 98, 106, 108, 122

L

Law of Action and Reaction, 75
Law of Cause and Effect, 75-77
Law of Restoration, 76
Law of the Harvest, 75-80, 82
Laying on of hands, 30, 121
Lectures on Faith, 114
Lee, Harold B., *Decisions for Successful Living*, 14
  on testimony, 14
Life of Heber C. Kimball (book), 14
Light, 15, 18, 29, 47, 54, 65, 92, 102,
  borrowed, 13, 14
  bringing forth, 9, 14, 19, 35, 124
  bringing up children in, 2, 6, 21, 23, 122
  of Christ, 40, 41, 63
  of the world, 63, 96
Lineage, divine, 26
  earthly, 26-29
Lion House, 6
Listening, during prayer, 97
Liverpool, England, 112
Logan Temple, 61
Lord's Question, The (book), 23, 41, 85
Los Angeles, California, 90
Love, 15, 44, 64, 104
  divine, 52, 64
  for God, 32, 53, 82, 115, 120
  for neighbor, 53
  for others, 47, 68, 75, 79, 85, 106
  in home, 6, 82
  of God, 16, 53
  scriptures on, 92-93
  unconditional, 54
  See also Caring; Charity; Compassion
Lowell, James Russell, "The Vision of Sir Launfal," 57-58
Lundwall, N. B., comp., *The Vision*, 115

M

Magazines, 1
Marriage, 82
  temple, 110
Melchizedek Priesthood holders, activity of, 68-69
Mental activity, 96-97
Michael, 28